The Synchromethod

The S/nchromethod

Dr. Hasai Aliev

The Synchromethod

A Key to New Heights of Inner Freedom, Stress Resistance and Creativity

Translated by Alison Yermolova

authorHOUSE®

AuthorHouse™ UK Ltd.
500 Avebury Boulevard
Central Milton Keynes, MK9 2BE
www.authorhouse.co.uk
Phone: 08001974150

First published by AuthorHouse 07/01/2011

ISBN: 978-1-4567-7911-5 (sc)
ISBN: 978-1-4567-7912-2 (e)

Contents

Contents

Foreword by Sergei Kolesnikov

The world has long been waiting for easy and fast-acting techniques for raising resistance to stress.

Rapid stress management skills are what everyone needs today when free time is at a premium, life is fast-paced, and tension runs high.

I became acquainted with Hasai Aliev more than 25 years ago, when, as a young budding scientist, he elicited the help of the Council of Young Scientists and Specialists of the Soviet Union to promote the broad application of the psychological discharge method he had developed for employees of industrial enterprises.

At that time, the method was successfully implemented at several defense enterprises of the microelectronics industry. Later, the method was substantially refined and formed the basis for several new methods.

The principles and techniques of the Key Anti-Stress Training differ from rehabilitation methods in that they make it possible to raise resistance to stress for successfully coping with any stressful situations you may encounter. People trained in the Key Method are level-headed, capable of quickly calming down, releasing inner tension, mobilizing their strength, relaxing, and recovering even as they carry on their daily tasks, that is, when faced with the stressful social, physical, and intellectual situations that accompany us every day.

With his Synchromethod, Dr. Hasai Aliev has made an invaluable contribution to contemporary psychotherapy and practical psychology, without which the development of these fields of science would not be the same today.

Sergei Kolesnikov, Deputy Chairman of the Russian Federation State Duma Health Care Committee, Academician of the Russian Academy of Medical Sciences. *Photo by Swedish photographer, Dennis Dahlqwist.*

Foreword by Gunilla Kleis

How to cope with stress and mobilize inner resources at any time and in any place.

If someone had told me eighteen months ago that I would be writing a letter to the President of Russia, I would have replied: "Me? Never! Why would I want to do that?" But I was wrong. When I was lucky enough to become acquainted with the simple and enlightening principles and techniques of the Synchromethod, they not only changed my life for the better, they made such an impression on me that I just had to write to President Medvedev and tell him that this unique method could also help other people.

"Dear Dmitri Anatolievich,

My name is Gunilla Kleis, I am a citizen of Finland and am writing to you regarding a very important issue.

I have long wanted to know how I might raise my personal efficiency without sacrificing my health, but I could never find the answer I was looking for.

As it turns out, the answer was right around the corner all the time, in Russia. And since I know Russian, I was able to acquaint myself with the only fast-acting anti-stress training method in the world, The Key, and its author Doctor Hasai Aliev.

Now I am translating Doctor Aliev's new book into Finnish and Swedish and hope that soon not only people in Scandinavia, but also throughout Europe will be practicing these unique techniques. Because the ability to handle stress is the foundation stone of human health and personal efficiency in any activity.

So, dear Mr. President, I am writing to you today to ask you to take part in creating a system that will enable the Russian population to learn stress resistance skills using this unique method and, along with Doctor Hasai Aliev, lay the foundation of a mental health system for Russia."

Let me tell you how all this came about.

Every spring I go with my friends on a hunting trip to the Arkhangelsk Region in the north of Russia. This week out in the countryside in the company of good friends has always been the best kind of vacation for me. There, in Russia's boundless and incredibly beautiful marshes, I am able to relax, forget about all my problems, and replenish my energy after a long and stressful winter.

One year, I was so exhausted and suffering from high blood pressure and a stomach ulcer that I was not up to going on my spring hunting trip. I was so disappointed.

But a good friend, a former colonel, encouraged me by saying: "Go ahead and come and I'll show a method that will help you not only to remove your stress but to always be able to control the way you feel, and everything will be just fine!"

This is how I first became acquainted with the Key's ideomotor techniques in the wild expanses of the Arkhangelsk Region. While everyone else went off to hunt, I stayed in the camp and "flew" over the marshes!

And not only did I "fly," I also discovered resources within me beyond my wildest dreams.

I just could not understand how I was able to do this with the help of such simple techniques, so, after I returned home rested from hunting, I immediately wrote a letter to Doctor Hasai Aliev in Russia and asked him to explain how his Key Method works.

Mr. Aliev invited me to come to Moscow and added, "You will see, Gunilla, that you do not always have to go to the marshes to remove stress and mobilize your resources, because you will be able to do this at any time and in any place."

Soon I found out that Doctor Aliev developed his Key Method as he worked with astronauts at the Gagarin Institute in Moscow, helping them to adapt to zero gravity conditions and training them in stress management skills.

Almost any conditions can be created on Earth, apart from weightlessness, which is usually simulated using the neutral buoyancy principle or by performing parabolic maneuvers in an especially equipped training aircraft. But since this kind of training is very expensive, Doctor Aliev began looking for similar mechanisms in other areas.

It soon became clear that Yogis practice something similar, which they call nirvana—a state of wellbeing accompanied by a feeling of weightlessness. But it takes long years of practice to reach this state.

After 30 years of research, Doctor Aliev discovered that this particular condition, which he calls a neutral state, is the foundation of all other health practices, only people did not know this. This is because it occurs spontaneously. In running, for example, it is called getting your second wind, in autogenic training, relaxation, in Oriental practice, meditation, and in religion, the blessing of prayer.

This state is achieved every time you engage in some activity and start to warm to your task, when you get in the rhythm and your movements becomes automatic. When this happens, your head clears, your body feels light, and everything you do takes the minimum amount of effort.

And this is all you need to eliminate stress, it is the Key to finding a state of being that allows you to manage your own inner resources. And you can reach this state here and now, right where you are. The Key Method allows you to achieve a feeling of weightlessness, or any other desirable state needed to solve your problems, all you need to do is choose the movements you find easiest to do, those that quickly become automatic.

"So why then are not all Russians practicing the Key?" I asked Doctor Aliev.

And he explained: "Because for ten years, this method was used exclusively for training army psychologists and special task forces sent to hot spots, for working with the personnel involved in raising the *Kursk* nuclear submarine, and for rehabilitating the victims, both children and adults, of the terrorist acts in Kaspiisk, Kizlyar, Essentuki, Moscow, and Beslan. And now the Key Method is being used to train the test pilots of the Mars-500 International Space Program."

Now you probably understand why I had to write to the President of Russia.

It is my sincere wish that the Key Method become available to everyone and the simple fast-acting Key techniques become part of the daily activity of every person, just as we brush our teeth every morning and evening to keep our teeth strong and healthy and have a beautiful smile!

Gunilla Kleis, Pietarsaari, Finland.

Preface from the Author

I want to help people of the East and West to better understand each other with the help of the Russian Synchromethod, which could only have appeared in Russia, a country situated at the crossroads between the West and the East and in search of a balance between material and spiritual values.

The 21st century is not only a technological, it is also a psychological age.

Human evolution occurs through the assimilation of energy—from mechanical to electric and nuclear energy, and now the highest of energies, the energy of stress. The future belongs to those people who can cope with stress, and this can be each and every one of us.

And do you know what the foundation stone of human health and personal efficiency in any activity is?

Resistant to stress! Even well-trained Olympic athletes can lose their bearings under stress and let that long-cherished medal slip from their hands.

This is because we learn in one state of consciousness, while the knowledge and skills we acquire must be applied in all kinds of different circumstances.

Raising our resistance to stress is the answer to solving difficult problems. It also reduces the need for medication, lowers accident risk and fatigue, raises learning ability, and increases self-confidence during exams, important business consultations, public speaking events, and in any other demanding or emergency situation, even those encountered in combat zones.

It is also invaluable during pregnancy and childbirth, making it possible for every future mother to give birth to a healthy and capable child.

Governor of Russia's Nizhny Novgorod Region Valery Shantsev and Professor Hasai Aliev discuss implementing a wide-scale project for raising resistance to stress. The first positive results have already been obtained—320 school teachers and 8,000 social workers trained in the method say they are very satisfied.

World chess champion Anatoli Karpov and Professor Hasai Aliev prepare a project for training athletes before the Olympic Games in Sochi.

THE SYNCHROMETHOD consists of:

1. A new model of brainwork
2. The Key Method—a unique self-regulation method based on ideomotor techniques and including the Key Stress Test for gauging how tense you are and increasing your ability to take successful action; and
3. Synchrogymnastics designed to quickly release inner tension, mobilize resources, restore strength, and develop creative capabilities and desirable qualities.

The method is particularly indispensible for people who push themselves to the limit either at home or at work, or in an urgent situation when you do not have the time or the conditions necessary to calm down, make a wise and rational decision, pull yourself together, and deal with the situation.

I sincerely hope that you will quickly find the Key to Yourself—a source of new strength and opportunities in your life!

Hasai Aliev is a Professor, Ph.D. (Medical Sciences), author of patents, Honored Doctor of the Republic of Daghestan, and General Director of the Moscow Stress Management Center.

Professor Hasai Aliev, author of the Synchromethod

Chapter 1.
The Key to Yourself

They say that time is money.
This is not true! Time is dearer than money,
Because we only have one life,
it passes never to return.

Hasai Aliev

In the 21st Century We Need Rapid Results

We live in a world of impetuous change.

At times of global transformation, value reappraisal, acute crises, information explosion, and natural disasters, when water is bottled, air is polluted, and medication can have unpredictable long-term effects, each of us needs some form of internal protection. And most important, we need inner freedom, without which no other freedom is possible.

The accelerated pace of contemporary life is putting our internal biological clock, which has been honed over millions of years of evolution, out of kilter. So we need to find appropriate responses to the challenges of the new times.

How can we find the key that opens the body's internal "apothecary," how can we manage these internal reserves? How can we tap the powerful creative potential that has been condensed in each of us over millions of years of evolution?

The Synchromethod, together with its Key Method and Synchrogymnastics, is based on previously unknown mechanisms of how the brain works that make it possible to achieve much more easily and rapidly the same results offered by other methods.

The Synchromethod is my way of helping my fellow men in our far-from-easy times and my answer to the new challenges of our evolution.

Key Method Is Innovative and Unique

The Key is the answer
for people who have no time.

Hasai Aliev

Every psychological method is aimed at solving psychological problems. And problems are solved when you have the clarity of mind and physical vitality to do what you need to do.

The Key Method is the quickest way in the world to achieve this: it brings the body into harmony with the mind, or, to put it scientifically, it coordinates the mental and physiological processes by synchronizing the activity of both hemispheres of the brain in the necessary direction.

There are many different psychological help and self-help programs designed to develop and enhance people's qualities and capabilities. So why do we need the Key?

We need the Key because the methods that exist, even such potent and effectual ones as Yoga, Qigong, Neuro-Linguistic Programming (NLP), and others, are not easily assimilated by the broad public and so cannot become a part of the general culture. This makes them of little use for quickly raising resistance to stress and developing the desired qualities and capabilities, since these methods require too much time, long years of perseverance, and a good teacher, at least.

If the Key had not been discovered, we would never have known that such sacral states as nirvana or enlightenment can be reached by each and every one of us at our own command. We would have still been under the illusion that this is the privilege of a chosen few who, by following one of the existing practices, have reached the supreme heights of higher vision through sheer persistence and long years of hard work on themselves, something which is beyond us ordinary mortals.

The purpose of these practices is indeed to improve health, raise mental stability, develop the ability to cope with stress, and achieve a state of inner and outer harmony, regardless of the situation that faces us.

However, I have developed a new model of brainwork which shows that all these different well-known practices are based on the same principles. My model reveals the rational kernel, the Key, that can be used in a simple compact form for reaching the most diverse goals.

With the help of the Key, you will be able to make the desirable changes in yourself, develop the qualities and abilities you wish, quickly understand your true desires, and make your dreams come true.

The Key is unique in that it removes stress automatically, since it works on the basis of reflexes.

The Key makes it possible to obtain the desired results when time is at a premium and you do not have suitable conditions for practicing other methods.

The Key is also unique in that it helps people who are unable or do not want to share their problems and concerns with a specialist.

The Key opens access to internal reserves that are usually only mobilized with unpredictable consequences in emergencies.

A case is known of a mother who lifted a heavy train carriage from the rails to save her child. Five men were unable to put it back in place.

So searching for ways to manage our internal reserves has been an important stage in the scientific development of human capabilities.

The new model of brainwork described in this book will help you to understand why, without special training, we cannot freely control the capabilities of our brains which are, however, activated not only in emergencies, but also with the help of psychotherapy, during hypnosis, for example.

The Key Method shows us how to manage our inner state in a short time and in conditions close to reality.

This is why it is of inestimable value and can help us solve the difficult problems we encounter in our lives. It is a method that sets us internally free.

It can help us manage our mental and physical reserves, activating them at will in the difficult circumstances of everyday life.

It is what each of us today needs.

This is important, for if we are unable to control ourselves, others will control us instead, and we will find ourselves in the grips of external circumstances and internal struggles.

3

The great Russian stage director Konstantin Stanislavsky, who is famous for his System of Acting, understood the importance of being relaxed when performing on stage. His message was clear and simple: you can't do 'inner work' if you are physically too tense. He proved his point when he asked his students to take turns lifting a piano and at the same time answer some relatively simple questions. While they were engaged in their physical exertion, they could not answer the questions, but as soon as they put the piano back down, the answers came easily.

Stanislavsky's genius was not only expressed in his ability to teach acting skills, but also in his understanding of the importance of inner freedom. He and his student, Mikhail Chekhov, taught actors to remove nervous tension caused by anxiety and stress, understanding that they were primarily blocks in consciousness.

The Key enables you to quickly find the inner state of wellbeing that will best help you to solve your problems.

This is very important!

Everyone knows that without inspiration, you cannot write poetry, and without mobilizing all your strength, you cannot accomplish that record-breaking jump.

Even at the Olympic Games, all other conditions being equal, the athletes best able to overcome stress are the ones who win. This is because stress prevents the mind from acting freely, drawing it into the mire of the current problem and holding it captive there.

Well-known Russian actor and film director Armen Dzigarkhanyan and Professor Hasai Aliev think that health and success are based on how you manage your internal state in life.

The Key makes it possible:

1. *To determine whether you are tense or ready to take successful action;*

2. *To quickly release inner tension ("a shot of courage" without alcohol);*

3. *To raise your efficiency in emergencies;*

4. *To activate additional reserves when solving difficult problems for finding ingenious solutions;*

5. *To switch from negative to positive thinking;*

6. *To control fear and pain;*

7. *To quickly restore your strength even without comfortable conditions;*

8. *To give yourself advice and, most important, carry it out;*

9. *To find better contact, even when talking to the most difficult partners;*

10. *To harmonize personal relations;*

11. *To discover hidden creative and other desirable capabilities;*

12. *To cure yourself of psychosomatic disturbances;*

13. *To get enough quality sleep;*

14. *To quickly reach a state of meditation, nirvana, relaxation, guided self-hypnosis.*

Therefore, the Key will primarily help you to rapidly release inner tension and, in so doing, raise your confidence and make it easier to manage your state of consciousness.

Can the Key help you to learn a foreign language or particular professional skills?

Who is better able to learn, assimilate a new profession, and adapt to new conditions? A tense or a relaxed person?

There is only one answer: a relaxed person!

The Key affords a rapid payoff and makes it easier for you to learn and train, improve your health, free yourself from any dependence, work on yourself, achieve the desirable results in any activity, and find the optimal solution to any problem you may face. It is also beneficial at the collective level, making it possible to optimize management and personnel relations at different levels in a corporation, raise labor productivity, and improve product quality.

The Two Basic Parts of the Key Method

1. The Key Stress Test

2. Easy Key techniques for managing the way you feel.

A regular five-minute Synchrogymnastics consisting of five short exercises of one minute each will help you to maintain an optimal level of creative and physical performance in any situation.

The Key Stress Test will help you to determine at any moment the level of your inner tension, whether you are under stress, tense, and need to relax, or, on the contrary, whether you are ready to go ahead and successfully perform what is required of you.

The Key Stress Test will also help you to determine how well you are coping with stress as you train with the Key or with any other exercises, just as a blood pressure monitor or thermometer helps you to measure your blood pressure or body temperature.

The Key will help you to rapidly reach a state of mobilization, freedom, balance, relaxation, and mediation, as well as an alert state of performance efficiency.

You will achieve the first clear results during the very first session. And each subsequent session will produce faster and faster results.

You will also be able to reach that special state known as nirvana, satori, or enlightenment, which, by using the well-known methods, usually takes months of intense training to achieve and requires a change in lifestyle and way of thinking.

The Key will help you to reach a state of nirvana in the simplest and easiest way, almost instantly, even in your own kitchen, without having to go to Tibet, for example.

This is because you already have all the resources you need within you.

It is important to note that along with the Key for regulating your inner state, you also get an effective 5-minute anti-stress health-improving workout based on the Key principles.

This limbering up before going into action is called Synchrogymnastics, the secret of which lies in the fact that the exercises offered are synchronized to the way you currently feel.

This new five-minute therapeutic super workout has the instant effect of setting you free accompanied by a feeling of relaxation, emotional uplift, and willingness to tackle things that previously seemed beyond you.

It consists of five simple techniques, the daily performance of which will put you in good creative and physical shape, regardless of your circumstances.

Synchrogymnastics help to effortlessly dissipate built-up negative emotions and tension and, in just five minutes, yield the same effect you would achieve from working out at a fitness club or swimming pool, or spending time at a health resort.

This is because these Synchrogymnastics immediately launch that therapeutic mechanism that is often spontaneously activated while running, skiing, doing aerobics, dancing, meditating, doing yoga or other exercises.

Synchrogymnastics have a high therapeutic effect and rid you of neurotic disorders, phobias, dependencies, and psychosomatic illnesses.

These simple contemporary exercises, which are very easy to perform, have been included in a new physical education textbook for upper classmen in Russia.

Personal Example
I suffered from severe bronchial asthma. I had 12-17 attacks of wheezing a day and could not turn from one side to the other in bed without a bout of coughing.

I was also laid up for about three months with acute back pain, and then had to wear a corset for six months.

Now, in the four years I have been regularly practicing Synchrogymnastics, I do not have any asthma attacks and I can easily bend and touch the floor. I do not take any medication.

Running ahead, I will also say that I discovered the artist in me using the Key Method, as many of my students have also done.

Easy Dance. The author

You can also use the five simple Synchrogymnastics techniques separately. It all depends on what you want to achieve.

For example, the Slapping Your Back technique helps you to loosen up and release inner tension. You can use it before any demanding or emergency situation to give you energy and boost your confidence. This exercise can be used for limbering up before going into action.

The Cross-Country Skier technique is beneficial for reaching an optimal creative state of emotional and physical equilibrium in order to make important decisions, since it quickly helps to focus your thoughts on what is troubling you, but with a calm rather than jumbled mind.

You can use the Twisting technique for Discharge and Recharge to activate the evolutionary mechanism nature has endowed us with in order to dissipate accumulated negative emotions and transfer to positive thinking. By performing this technique at intervals and regulating the number of minutes you practice it, you can also use it as a Mill for pulverizing any psychological trauma or problem situation, or as a soothing and relaxing Lullaby before going to bed in order to achieve better-quality sleep. That is what your mother did when she rocked you in her arms when you were a baby.

The other two Synchrogymnastics exercises, Bending and Easy Dance, have their own special features and possibilities.

A full description of all these techniques and instructions for doing them can be found in Chapter 8 "Synchrogymnastics."

A New Approach—A Paradoxical Conclusion and Unique Technique for Raising Stress Resistance

One and the same problem may give rise to different amounts of tension depending on how critical the problem is and the internal resources you have available to deal with it.

For example, if you have a ready algorithm for solving the task, tension will be minimal, if not, the brain, like an automatic self-regulator, raises the tension, which sends out more energy to search for the necessary information in its depositories and channel it in the right direction.

You will find out how the search processes are carried out at the level of the psyche when you read the chapter that describes the new model of brainwork, but for now I will give an example of how insufficient reserves take their toll at the physiological level.

You have not had enough sleep, for example, and the brain automatically raises tension to increase the blood flow in order to supply its cells with more oxygen.

This mobilizing work to supply resources is carried out by the valve system of the blood vessels and neck muscles, which contract and relax like a pump.

In so doing, the muscles may go into spasms and, in the event of chronic tension, osteochondrosis arises, which creates a rigid block to the flow of resources.

This is why many people often suffer from neck pain.

And this in itself is a block.

What must the brain do to ensure the cells are provided with enough oxygen when there is a block in the way?

The brain must raise the tension even more in order to overcome the block and deliver oxygen to its destination.

So the same problem you easily solved yesterday could become stressful today because of the disparity between the critical nature of the task to be solved and the resources available to solve it, in other words, because of a lack of coordination between the mind and body.

From this we can see why the brain's reserve capabilities, which we usually have no control over, are often activated in emergencies. High tension can sometimes break through both physiological and psychological blocks.

For example, after an emotional shock, clinical death experience, or some other extremely distressing situation, one person may begin painting, while another discovers his or her music skills or other capabilities.

The Key Method is a "peaceful way" to attain high achievements, a way that removes blocks by teaching how to release tension.

It is a way to acquire experience, wisdom, and self-perfection without extreme tension and emotional shocks.

It is a way to manage the reserves that used to be spontaneously activated only at levels of critical tension.

It is my answer to the cherished question of how to manage our internal reserves.

The truth lay on the surface, and many have been approaching it from different angles, but it was difficult to see that such different phenomena as the extraordinary things achieved during emergencies, hypnosis, and relaxation exercises are all based on the same mechanism—removing blocks.

Now we understand that the only way to open up our potential capabilities is to learn how to remove blocks!

Many beneficial practical conclusions ensue from this idea.

Here is an example.

One of the basic conditions of self-confidence is the ability to keep your neck muscles relaxed at the critical moment.

How do we usually learn to release the tension in our muscles?

We are usually trained how to relax our muscles in comfortable conditions, for example, in a relaxed position, either sitting or lying down, perhaps with the use of massage, reflexotherapy, or other methods.

However, this kind of training is utterly useless if you want to learn how to deal with future emergencies. For someone who is learning how to raise their resistance to stress in order to cope with future stressful situations, learning to relax in comfortable conditions is not training, but de-training, since comfortable conditions and artificial relaxation techniques decrease the ability to keep the neck muscles relaxed in tense situations.

> **In order to raise your ability to deal with stress and your personal efficiency in tense situations, you need to train in conditions close to reality.**
>
> **This is the principle of anti-stress training.**

A relaxed pose, comfortable conditions, massage, reflexotherapy, and similar techniques serve a different purpose; they are beneficial for rehabilitation, that is, for restoring the body after it has been through stressful situations.

A state of tension characteristic of stressful situations is simulated using the Key Method by assuming an uncomfortable body position that you hold for a short time, for example, a half-bridge.

Try bending slightly backwards in an arc.

You can regulate the amount of tension by the degree to which you bend your body—the further you bend backwards, the higher the tension will be.

Remember the amount of tension that arises as you do this.

And now, while holding this uncomfortable tense pose, begin loosening up your neck muscles by moving your head slightly back and forth, as though freeing your neck from its joint. Try to find the most relaxing movements, bending your head from left to right, for example, turning it, or doing some other releasing movements.

Notice how your tension immediately decreases. Now you can bend backwards even further. It is amazing! But in actual fact, all you have done is shift your attention, so the original task becomes easier, and the tension-releasing movements have improved your blood flow.

Recall how you do approximately the same thing when you wake up in the morning. You stretch, tensing up your muscles, extending your arms, and moving your head back and forth, in so doing, instinctively doing anti-stress exercises.

Like this exercise, all the other Synchrogymnastics exercises are also built on our natural self-regulation mechanisms.

By doing this exercise to raise stress resistance for just one minute a day, you can develop your ability to keep a clear mind and boost your confidence in any difficult and tense situation.

You can read the complete instructions on how to perform this Bending exercise and the other unique Key exercises in the chapters called "How to Choose the Key to Yourself" and "Synchrogymnastics."

Chapter 2.
The Key Stress Test

*When a person is internally free, he is guided
by his reason and a feeling of harmony, whereas
when he is tense he is controlled by fear, complexes,
stereotypes...and other people's advice.*
                                        Hasai Aliev

Effective From the Word Go

If you work at the computer you will easily understand this concept.

You know what freezing up means, when you press the keys, but nothing happens, the screen does not react.

Something like freezing up happens in the human brain when it is under stress. Signals come in, but the brain does not react, it has "frozen." This is why you often do not realize you are under stress, and so you are unable to solve your problem.

Our Key Stress Test is designed to help you gage your current state and recognize the symptoms that indicate you are under stress.

From the Television Archives

An aerospace forces officer participating in one of the Key training courses was unhappy with his results. All the participants in the training session quickly got the hang of the Key techniques, but he was having problems.

The Key Stress Test showed he had a high level of nervous psychic tension.

Then he did the Synchrogymnastics techniques, sat down and suddenly, with one leg crossed over the other, turned toward the other participants and exclaimed unselfconsciously:

"I understand why I can't do the Key exercises! My son is getting married in two weeks and my wife and I are constantly wondering where we're going to get the money for the wedding, how we're going to entertain the guests. I've been so hung up on that. And now after doing these exercises, I sat down and thought, "We're not the first to be in this situation, it happens to lots of people. We'll find the money, we'll invite our guests, and everything will be just fine!"

"I'm not hung up anymore!"

For the First Time—A Test with Feedback

Biofeedback or BFS is a technical system used to monitor and consciously regulate many of the body's automatic functions.

The sensors of an electroencephalograph, electrocardiograph, electromyograph, or some other device are hooked up to the body to register the activity of its organs and systems. This equipment alerts you to any changes going on in your body and consequently enables you both to track the problem areas and promote an improvement in your inner wellbeing.

However, to use a biofeedback system, you need to have access to the machine and know how to hook it up properly; and it can be relatively expensive. The main shortcoming of this technical system is that it is only good for reducing the physical effects of stress or relieving the symptoms of certain disorders, it does not teach you how to manage your inner wellbeing, never mind your creative resources.

The special feature of our Key Stress Test is that you can, with its help, wherever you are, both check you own wellbeing and regulate it, that is, improve your wellbeing.

The Key techniques used in the Stress Test remove stress automatically and activate self-control, the advantages of which you will discover in this book.

And all of this can be done without the use of special equipment.

To be more exact, your own hands, feet, head, and body play the role of these instruments as you perform the ideomotor techniques. Even the movements of your finger can be used as a BFS device.

If you are in a state of internal equilibrium, which means you are capable of controlling yourself and the situation you are in, you will be able to do the Key techniques, if not, you can reduce your stress and remove your tenseness by repeating these Key techniques until you reach the desired state.

So the Key techniques simultaneously allow you to control and regulate your wellbeing.

The Key Stress Test Is Based on Two Phenomena

1. the ability to focus your attention;

2. the emergence of a reflex reaction in response to an image.

For example, the vivid image of a lemon might push out all other thoughts and cause the body to respond with the customary reflex— salivation. In the same way, other vivid images can arouse reflex reactions. For example, the passenger in a car involuntarily steps down on an imaginary brake peddle when the traffic light turns to red.

The same reactions can also be aroused from a less vivid image. But the main criterion is the same—you need to keep your mind free from extraneous thoughts.

If you are feeling stressed, you will not be able to remove irrelevant thoughts and bring about the desirable reaction. For example, you tell yourself before an exam, "Keep calm!" but your heart does not obey, it beats wildly in your chest.

In other words, the Key Stress Test determines whether you are able to focus your attention, and the reflex is confirmation of this.

The test is unique in that it not only checks for the presence or absence of stress, but also simultaneously removes it. This happens because there is a changeover in the dominant foci in the brain, just like switching gears when driving a car.

And now try the Key Stress Test for yourself!

Do You Want to Learn How to Fly?

Imagine that your arms, which are stretched out before you, begin moving in opposite directions without any effort on your part, automatically.

Alicia doing the Key Stress Test

Don't rush, live with this exercise for 10-20 seconds.

The main thing here is your desire, which will come to pass if you expel all superfluous thoughts from your head.

The more internally calm you are, the easier this is to do.

Choose an image to help you, for example, imagine that your arms are pushing away from each other, like unipolar magnets.

After this, let your arms drop, while imagining that they immediately begin to levitate again, rising up in opposite directions.

Visualize your arms floating up effortlessly, like wings, like fluff, like an astronaut hovering in space.

Maybe while you are doing this you will begin to feel your body swaying slightly. Excellent! You should try to encourage this; just let yourself go. Do not be afraid! No one ever falls. You can place your feet further apart if you like.

This automatic swaying of the body shows that you are entering a state of so-called mental relaxation. Allow your body to sway in a pleasant rhythm, like a tree in the wind. While you do so, the feeling of inner peace, lightness, weightlessness, flight, that is, levitation, grows.

This entire Test procedure may take no more than five minutes.

Approximately 70% of people are able to shed their tension and reach a state of inner freedom accompanied by a feeling of flying and nirvana the very first time they try the Test. In so doing, they restore their inner balance and set their minds on achieving the desired results—the personal and life changes they wish to bring about. This book will show you how to accomplish this, and you will experience a qualitative improvement in your life.

If the Key Stress Test shows you are tense, you can release your tension another way, by using the additional techniques and exercises described in the section called Synchrogymnastics, which are tension-releasing techniques. They are designed to help you unwind and raise your ability to manage your wellbeing, which will be of extraordinary benefit to you!

When you first try the Key Stress Test, it is best to sit down after you have finished and just sit, resting, regardless of the direct results of the Test.

This is the Aftereffect Stage. The Moment of Truth, when you begin to feel the changes that have occurred in you after performing the Test.

At this Stage, if you sit still for several minutes, intensive rehabilitation occurs with the emergence of a sense of mental and physical wellbeing, as though you are experiencing something immensely delightful.

During the Aftereffect Stage, it is not necessary at all to make a special effort to relax or drive thoughts out of your mind.

It is recommended you do the following:

1. Keep your eyes still (do not shift them from one object to another). Keep your eyes open at first, but unfocused, with your gaze vacant, as though looking into the middle distance. Do not close your eyes until you feel you need to.

2. Let your thoughts run free, let random thoughts come into your mind, and do not drive away any unpleasant thoughts, just allow thoughts to come as they will.

3. If you become sleepy, teary, or your head feels empty, do not do anything to prevent this discharging process.

After a few minutes, the desired feeling of peace and well-being will come upon you. Perhaps you will first experience discharge—you might relive past experiences, followed by a burst of renewal. You are already reacting differently to the same experiences, you see them much more calmly.

The main thing is not to rush.

While resting, you need to wait for the moment when your head clears and you feel an inflow of renewed energy, then open your eyes and stretch as you would after a good night's sleep.

Frequently your vision becomes sharper, objects become more distinct, and colors brighter.

This usually takes from one to ten minutes, or perhaps, if you are extremely fatigued, half an hour or even a whole hour. Take your time. You will know when it is time to open your eyes.

You will feel like you would after a brisk walk or nap in the fresh air, full of renewed strength and energy.

Doing this exercise one time may have the same restorative effect on the body as is achieved after spending a month at a health resort.

The Key Stress Test shows you whether or not you can immediately use the Key techniques to reach the inner equilibrium required for making positive changes in yourself, or whether you first need to try some tension-releasing techniques, or even Discharge and Recharge.

The girl does not want to participate in the discussion, she looks skeptical. Why?

The Stress Test shows that she is under stress. After doing the Key exercises for a few minutes, her arms begin to move apart. The stress has been removed!

Here's the result! Balance has been restored.

Chapter 3.
Stress Is Not Tension

When resolving any problem, you come up
against yourself, against your internal problems.
Stress prevents you from seeing the world in its
entirety and from activating your inner resources.
By managing stress, you manage your life.

Hasai Aliev

If the human brain is the most perfect universal and fastest-acting system in nature with incredible capabilities, why do we feel stress?

And why is it usually said that we use only 5-10 percent of our brains?

Is this perhaps because some of the brain's capabilities are only designed to cope with emergencies?

But this is not true!

Stress occurs because some of the brain's capabilities are blocked.

Fears, complexes, and stereotypes that begin forming from early childhood due to inadequate learning and upbringing and negative experiences cause psychological blocks.

How does this happen?

Children are active and curious, so they are often kept in check; children learn and their behavior is evaluated. They are more often told "no" and "don't do that" than praised for good conduct. They often hear that nothing is gained without great effort, that you must study hard with your nose to the grindstone, nothing comes easy, creativity has a high price, and so on.

This creates blocks—ideas about our limited capabilities.

The blocks may be caused by physiological disturbances, for example, muscle spasms, poor blood circulation that does not provide the brain with enough oxygen, and so on.

Blocks prevent the brain from adapting in the way that is needed to achieve an integrated perception of the world and activate inner resources, and this restricts our ability to think creatively and undermines our health.

When we come up against a block
during a situation we encounter or
when we face some problem, our level
of tension automatically rises. We have
no control over it, and this is called
stress.

Stress Is Overtension

Once when I announced at a military academy that we would be learning
how to remove stress, the university president, a general, asked, "You
mean relax? But what if a tank is bearing down on a soldier?"

That is when I realized that I needed to choose my words more
carefully.

We are used to calling any type of tension stress, while removing
stress means unwinding, slacking off, relaxing.

I remember how many years ago the phrase "a shot [of vodka] for
courage" was all the rage. This is what young boys said before they went
on their first date. And it echoes back to the war when soldiers were
given a shot of vodka before they went into an attack.

So we are used to thinking that a small dose of relaxation means
removal of inhibition, removal of tension, mobilization. Whereas a large
dose of relaxation, well I don't need to tell you where that might lead.

So one and the same process, removing tension, could generate
an increase in energy and boost in confidence, while in most cases
this process means relaxation, sluggishness, and a lowered response to
signals.

So the general was partly right.

The confusion arises since the term *stress* in the English language
is used to cover both the positive and negative connotations of this
phenomenon.

Ever since Hans Selye, who developed a theory of stress, called the
characteristic syndrome observed in various illnesses stress, all problem
states began to be called stress, and this has given rise to the endless
discussions about the harm and possible benefits caused by stress.

In actual fact, stress is always harmful.

Whereas tension is another matter.

Tension is a natural and normal state, without which there can be no mobilization of the resources a person needs to resolve a particular problem.

You cannot climb a mountain, for example, without tension, i.e. the ability to exert yourself. Creative people appreciate the benefits of tension. It is a natural stage in the creative process of problem-solving.

So your health and success depend on your ability to deal with the tension created when problems need to be solved.

Stress is not tension!

Stress is overtension of the body's regulatory systems.

It is a state in which you lose control of yourself and the situation at hand.

You can determine whether you are experiencing stress by asking yourself: can I think about what I want at the moment or will my thoughts switch back to the topic bothering me?

Stress begins when you are unable to freely focus your attention.

Example

A patient came to see me. We sit and talk. She seems to understand everything we are talking about, she nods her head.

But does she really understand? Nodding the head may not mean total understanding.

Then she did some of the Key exercises, her tension lifted, and suddenly she raised her head and said:

"Oh, you have a picture on the wall!"

"What, you never noticed it before?!"

But how can we see, hear, and understand when we are under stress, our brains are fighting to overcome the tension, and our attention is restricted?

When we are stressed, our thoughts are jumbled, and our attention is restricted because it is fixed on the stressor, which focuses our thoughts on a possible negative outcome of the situation.

This phenomenon is usually called tunnel vision, a mechanism that I call "freezing up" in this book.

Freezing up gives rise to nervous muscle spasms. They, in turn, prevent us from diverting our attention. So a viscous circle is created—a state of tenseness.

It comes as no surprise that this state is caused by the brain's adaptation response, which when under stress warns you about the possible negative outcomes of the situation you are in, thus preparing you to take any necessary action.

For example, you went up onto the roof and suddenly it began raining. Your brain generates possible scenarios that mobilize you; your feet may slip and you will be unable to hold on, so you slide off the roof. These are warning signals to prepare you for the action you must take in such circumstances. If you are able to cope with stress, you can take advantage of these warnings and act efficiently, if not, tension builds until it becomes overtension, your attention becomes fixed on these images, and, in a trance, you could fall under their influence as though hypnotized and become the victim of your own overly active imagination.

When you experience stress, your resources may either be activated, sometimes even ensuring the best outcome, or they may be blocked.

For example, you are standing in front of a high fence and wondering whether or not you can jump over it. But a ferocious dog is running after you and you scale that fence in an instant! Because the dog has expelled all doubts. Otherwise it will tear your pants!

So you can!

High tension eliminated the psychological barriers, those doubts related to stereotypical thinking and ideas about yourself and your limited capabilities.

In some cases, when under stress, a person is capable of manifesting extraordinary capabilities by freeing himself from mental blocks under the effect of a critical level of tension. But this is fraught with unpredictable consequences.

So we need tension-releasing techniques that guarantee we achieve our goals and acquire inner freedom before we reach a state of critical tension.

This is what the Key Method is all about!

Release from Tension and Relaxation

Release from tension is not relaxation but removal of mental blocks and a sense of freedom!

Release from tension activates our inner resources, focuses our attention, forms the foundation of positive thinking, and forges the ability to look for a solution and not become hung up on failure.

Relaxation, on the other hand, means reaching a passive state with a sluggish reaction to signals. Relaxation means being sluggish.

This is because the brain is concentrating not on expending energy, but on restoring it.

My clarification of the concepts of stress, tension, relaxation, and release from tension is a very important turning point in the history and development of practical psychology.

Confusing the concepts of release from tension and relaxation even led Schultz, the author of the well-known method of autogenic training, who dreamed of creating a system that would enable people to control the way they feel without the assistance of or being dependent on a hypnotizer, to consequently develop a method of relaxation in conditions isolated from reality in a passive pose, while we need a method that will create inner freedom.

The Key Is a New Effective Method against Burnout

Sleep on it, your legs can't do the walking when your head is doing too much 'talking.'
Hasai Aliev

People usually come to see psychologists in order to tell them all about their problems and receive helpful recommendations. Sometimes it is very difficult for psychologists to listen for hours on end to the trials and tribulations of their patients. And it is often very difficult for the patients themselves to talk about what is troubling them.

I teach psychologists that first it is better to encourage patients to calm down and help them to see how they can remove stress themselves, rather than give advice.

I tell my patients that I am willing to give them my full attention, but first they must perform a test.

I place a clock before them and suggest they sway in a comfortable rhythm for 5-10 minutes, allowing their thoughts to flow as they will. As they do this, I keep an eye on them while taking care of other business. This technique not only helps patients to remove their stress, but also helps me to retain my equilibrium.

Soon the mechanical swaying becomes automatic. I ask my patients to sit down and remain sitting for 2-3 minutes, letting thoughts flow as they will and allowing their gaze to remain unfocused, as though looking into the middle distance.

Then I take a piece of paper and pencil, move my chair closer, and ask: "What are your problems?"

And the usual response is, "What problems? I don't think I have any problems, my head is empty! Certain thoughts wander in, but nothing that bothers me. I don't feel like reacting."

This phenomenon is called emotional distancing, so-called detachment, contemplation, when thoughts and emotions are separate. Sometimes the head really is empty!

The patient has reached a state of mental and physical equilibrium.

Sometimes in this state, a particular topic surfaces that has been buried deep in the subconscious and has kept the patient unwittingly under stress.

By allowing it to surface, automatic psychoanalysis has occurred.

Then I discuss this topic with my patient in order to formulate an action plan that will help him or her to solve the task themselves with the help of the Key techniques.

Sometimes a patient comes up against a block, or painful topics surface that have been pushed out of the mind and now emerge with a feeling of discomfort and depression. This is when Discharge and Recharge must be performed.

However, other patients who come with more complex problems, want to cure themselves of some ailment, or raise their professional skills, for example, require greater attention. Depending on the complexity of the problem, several sessions may be required and an individual program designed accompanied by brief consultations by phone or via the Internet.

So the first task of the psychologist is to help patients calm down and find their own positive attributes. This does not require a lot of time or questioning them at length about their problems, because the Key is a psychophysiological method and, after the mind has been brought into harmony with the body, they are able to resolve all their problems themselves.

This is one of the advantages of the Key.

An Amazingly Simple Technique to Unwind

This excellent tension-releasing exercise called Rocking is similar to when a mother rocks her baby in her arms.

I used this technique to draw a group of 140 victims simultaneously out of their state of shock within the space of three hours after the terrorist act in Beslan. When the swaying of their bodies became automatic, I knew they had begun to unwind, and I asked them to sit down. And there was a deluge of tears. Discharge had occurred, followed by a sigh of relief and the words: "O, at last I feel release, why didn't we do this before?!"

An Amusing Example

Here we have a large strong corpulent man. He was Chairman of the Russian Olympic Committee at the time. He complained that he had to take a handful of pills every night to fall asleep. I asked him to stand up and sway back and forth, or spin this way and that.

"What for?" he asked.

"You'll see!" I said, "that's how a mother rocks her baby."

A few seconds later, a snore was heard, he jumped, and shook himself.

"What, did I fall asleep?" he asked in amazement. "Why doesn't everyone do this?"

"Because they don't know about it! And they can't believe that something difficult can be achieved so easily."

When choosing the Key techniques that suit you best, this kind of rocking comes as a natural choice. Automatic swaying of the body is a sign of winding down. And by consciously rocking, you can help yourself to unwind.

Begin by mechanically swaying forward and backward, or try circular movements, for example.

This technique is simple: stand and rock gently back and forth, and think about whatever comes to mind. Imagine you are standing in a moving bus or train, the train is moving and rocking you.

If you feel more comfortable, you can fold your arms over your chest.

If you are tense, it will be difficult to keep your eyes closed.

And you do not have to close them immediately.

On the contrary, it is better to keep your eyes open at first, you can close them as soon as you feel the need.

Do what is easiest for you, you do not need to make any effort to relax, this will happen automatically. It will become easier and easier to rock, because tension is dropping away naturally.

Or you can try the following: pay attention to your inner voice, where is it pulling you? Let yourself go in that direction.

The main thing is to find a rhythm you enjoy. It should be a rhythm you want to keep on doing indefinitely, without stopping.

When you find it and reach the point where you do not want to stop, it means you have found your Accommodating Biorhythm, a rhythm in which your mental and physiological processes coincide.

In so doing, a feeling of profound mental and physical peace arises, a feeling of internal equilibrium.

Or you may achieve this state of being using a different technique.

Can you remember spreading your arms as you lay on your back in the water and were rocked by the waves? Try it. Throw your head back slightly, spread out your arms. Relax.

You will not fall. No one ever falls!

Remember this feeling.

You are now acquiring the ability to reach a state of mental and physical equilibrium without rocking at all.

Consequently, you also lose your fear of falling. And a person who was afraid of falling and now no longer fears he will fall are two completely different people!

Heaven and Earth
Three workers who have come from the village are sitting on a couch in the office of my brother Shamil. My brother introduces me to them, telling them that I am the doctor they may have seen on television.

"We don't watch television," one of them said, "we have no time for television."

"You see! They have no time for learning, they work, they are busy earning a living, try explaining to them why they need self-control!"

I asked them: "When you pray, do you find that extraneous thoughts interfere?"

"They shouldn't!" one replied.

"I know they shouldn't," I piped in, "but do they interfere or not?"

"I struggle with them," was the reply, "sometimes they creep into my head: about my family, about the things I have to do."

But the Prophet said that when you pray you must not think about other things. Now there is a way to learn how to fulfill the Prophet's commandment. I asked the worker to stand up and close his eyes, relax the muscles of his body. When he had relaxed, his body began swaying and he was immediately put on his guard. I asked him to find a pleasant rhythm to sway to, one that was not tiring but that he enjoyed. I told him that no one fell while doing this, and that even children could do it. A minute later, his face relaxed and his breathing became even.

"And now, after you've finished this exercise, sit down and just sit for a minute in silence," I requested.

He sat down and a few seconds later, a smile of amazement spread across his lips. A kind of lightness had filled his body, he said, and his head, he said, had become empty, devoid of any disturbing thoughts, as though he had just had a good night's sleep.

"If you do that several times, for five minutes a day, say, you will know how to remove tension and expel unnecessary thoughts from your head without the help of these exercises, use this to focus your mind and heart, and Allah will hear your prayer!"

Chapter 4.
The Key Is Choosing the Movement that Best Harmonizes with the Way You Currently Feel

Wisdom comes from equilibrium

Hasai Aliev

In order for words to have an effect, they must be carefully chosen to comply with the person's perception. So psychological methods are difficult since they require good knowledge of the culture and mentality of the person, of his or her individual characteristics and world outlook, internal image of the world, unresolved problems, and so on. And what if the person speaks a different language, or is of a different faith, or of an entirely different culture, or perhaps we are dealing with a child?

A case is known when a psychotherapist suggested that a patient relax by imagining the smooth surface of a blue lake, but instead she had hysterics—as a child she had almost drowned in a lake. And if she has the nervous jitters, how will she be able to relax by following the advice to think about something "calming"?

My favorite image is of Adriano Celentano in the movie *The Taming of the Shrew* who chops wood all night to calm his amorous passions, he's in love.

But imagine him being able to relax if a psychologist suggested the traditional approach, asking him to sit or lie comfortably and relax in meditation.

This is difficult to do without preliminary training. As you see, in this example there is no correspondence between the way the person is feeling and the action suggested to remove tension.

I can give another example that fails to ensure correspondence between current emotions and the action suggested. This is autogenic training.

The well-known autogenic training method asks you to sit comfortably or lie down and relax, then imagine a feeling of warmth and heaviness in your arms and legs and throughout your entire body in order to arouse mental relaxation.

33

But imagine that a person has cold hands and feet. He has vegetative-vascular dystonia. Come on now, he must learn to control it! But how can a person arouse warmth in his body if hands are cold?

And what will happen in these comfortable conditions if you have not had enough sleep? You will simply fall asleep!

What if you are emotionally overexcited?

Naturally, you will be unable to relax. You need more active movements.

The gist of the Key Method lies in choosing the movement that corresponds to the way you are currently feeling.

You experienced the benefit of this approach when you were a infant.

Your mother picked you up and rocked you.

And you calmed down.

Attention!

A child calms down regardless of the reason he or she was crying, whether the cause was psychological, someone took away his toy, for example, or physiological, she had a stomach ache.

The main thing is that a result is achieved if this rocking corresponds to the way the child is currently feeling.

Otherwise, if the mother is not in tune with her child's emotional state, if she is under stress herself, she will "shake" him so hard that he won't be able to relax.

On the other hand, if the child is more tense, he should be rocked more frequently—the higher the tension, the higher the frequency of the necessary repetitive movement.

This is why, for example, adolescents like hard rock, while older people take a greater liking to classical music.

The more the movement corresponds to the way you are currently feeling, the greater its freeing effect will be.

> **Movement that best harmonizes with the way you currently feel produces an instantaneous freeing effect, and when repeated, it leads to relaxation.**

But how can you determine your current state of being at any point in time?

How can you do this without special equipment and other auxiliary means?

And how can you best choose the movement that removes stress, the movement that opens up access to control over your inner wellbeing?

You Instinctively Look for That Internal Balance

My friend John from Canada told me that his feet move back and forth whenever he is sitting at his desk and concentrating on writing a document. If he tries to keep them still, he loses his concentration.

"Is that normal?" John asked me.

"That's the way the body is designed," I replied, "if there is concentration in one place, there is relaxation in another. This is the mechanism that helps the body to find a balance. Find the Key to yourself and you will be able to concentrate without superfluous movements."

When a person is nervous, he paces to and fro, rocks back and forth his chair, swings his leg, or drums his fingers on the table.

You can recall many similar examples yourself.

When it encounters stress, the body produces an anti-stress defense reaction.

Repetitive movement is one of the ways the body regulates itself, this movement is performed automatically; when you are nervous, it is easier to do than not to do.

A mother tells her child: "Stop swinging your leg!"

She is right of course; it is not polite to swing your leg in public.

But how are you supposed to cope with your tension?

That is why rock and roll, chewing gum, prayer beads, and much more based on the principle of repetitive relaxing movements have become popular in the world.

Repetitive movement means alternating tension and relaxation designed to find a state of inner equilibrium.

A nervous tick or an athlete who experiences prestart jitters, for example.

The higher the tension, the higher the frequency of the repetitions.

The brain keeps unbalanced internal systems in balance by raising the frequency of repetition when tension is high.

A stutterer, for example, repeats syllables and, in so doing, compensates for the lack of coordination between the speed at which the speech signal passes in the two halves of the brain.

Obsessively churning thoughts over in your head, having a certain song on the brain, and nervous ticks, are all part of the adaptive anti-stress defense syndrome.

Boxers in the ring dance about not only to distract their opponent, but also to remove the tension that is accumulating.

This is why a person's hands shake when he has a hangover, it is a defense reaction of the brain aimed at restoring balance.

The higher the tension, the higher the frequency of the repetitive action.

For example, when physical exertion increases, respiration quickens and the heart beats faster.

These are adaptation mechanisms. The body brings its internal systems into harmony with each other by alternating tension and relaxation and regulating the frequency of repetitive movements depending on the level of tension.

Repetitive prayer is associated with the same natural adaptation mechanism of the brain aimed at coordinating the mental and physiological processes. But these laws governing brainwork are not usually taken into account, because, for example, prayers are addressed to God, while swinging the legs is associated with the body.

I was holding a training session in the Key Method with a group of test pilots of the international Mars 500 space program before their eighteen months of isolation in order to carry out full flight imitation of a trip to Mars. During the training, I asked them to stand up, relax, think of some stressful situation, and observe what movements they would like to perform instead of relaxing.

One of the test pilots began jerking his arms and legs slightly like a boxer getting ready to fight. It turned out that he was indeed a boxer. And he liked exercising with his skipping rope, jumping quickly over the rope. He was happy to know that these movements and rhythms suited him for relaxation, and he could use them without the skipping rope.

Another test pilot began reproducing effortless swimming movements.

That's right, he liked swimming and found time spent in the swimming pool relaxing.

Each of the test pilots demonstrated his own special traits, which later helped them to quickly choose the Key techniques best suited to them individually.

It often happens that a person becomes a boxer, or skier, or drummer who finds the movements associated with the corresponding activity the easiest and quickest way to relax.

This is an effective way to make career choices.

And what about gesticulations! After all, these are actions that accompany the images which arise in our minds during reflection. They are a mechanism for coordinating mental and physical processes. If your hands are bound, you are unable to think as clearly.

Nervous automatic repetitive movements are generated by basic brain processes which physiologists call excitement and slowdown. The body uses this alternating ying-yang to achieve internal equilibrium—harmony.

These laws governing brainwork serve as the basis for creating the Key techniques—movements which correspond maximally to a person's current state of being and so activate coordination of the internal systems.

But what movement corresponds maximally to a person's current state? What are the criteria for choosing the techniques and exercises that remove tension and create feedback with our current state in order to control the body?

How do you choose shoes in a store? You pick the pair that fits you, the shoes that do not pinch. The ones that are your size!

Attention!

The movement you choose is the one that requires the least effort to perform.

What movement can you do without any effort at all?

What movement comes automatically? This is the movement that is right for you.

So the criterion governing the individual choice of movement for removing stress is the degree to which the movement is automatic and how quickly it becomes automatic.

For example, swinging your arms or swaying your body, or, ideally, a ideomotor movement that is performed automatically at any moment you wish! You asked for it—you got it! That means it corresponds to your current state. This is why ideomotor techniques remove stress automatically.

Why do we need to simulate these automatic movements if swinging the arms or legs removes tension?

Why can't we simply sway back and forth?

Because although swinging your leg may remove tension, it does not teach you anything.

By learning how to choose movements that synchronize with your current state, you will learn to manage your wellbeing without these movements.

So you should choose a movement depending on how willing your body is to perform it. It is no secret that smashing plates helps to reduce stress. Because this action does not require any effort. This is why it is usually easier for people to take medication than work on themselves. However, the Key Method teaches us how to control our inner state. And so that you can make use of it, it is based on the same principle— achieving a rapid result with the least effort.

Do your muscles tense up when you are under stress?

If so, it follows logically that in order for them to relax, they must first be tensed up even more.

Edmund Jacobson's well-known Progressive Relaxation Technique is based on this principle.

Incidentally, if this technique is viewed from the perspective of the Key's natural principles, it is easier to explain to the newcomer how to correctly perform the exercises if he is asked to think about he tenses up his muscles when stretching in the morning after getting up. There he does it in an even more natural way.

And if you have nervous jitters, logically you should shake yourself like kids at a discotheque.

One of the Key's quick and simple warm-up and tension-releasing techniques, Ideomotor Vibrogymnastics, created by my son and student, Allen Aliev, is based on this principle.

And if you want to shake off your depression, or improve your sleep, and you are tossing and turning about in bed unable to fall asleep, you can use the Twisting technique (described in Chapter 8) that brings about discharge.

I am proud to say that this technique was created by my daughter and student, Sheila Alieva.

Psychologist Allen Aliev

Psychologist Sheila Alieva with her daughter Greta, a future psychologist

Chapter 5.
Discharge and Recharge Are the Foundation of Good Health and Creativity

There are many different problems in the world, and each seems to require its own solution, but there is one thing that will solve any problem, no matter how difficult it be, and that is a clear head.

Hasai Aliev

I am convinced that an evolutionary adaptive Discharge and Recharge mechanism functions in the brain that helps the body to restore its internal balance at an increasingly higher level depending on the challenges it encounters and the demands of evolution.

This mechanism makes it possible for us to remove tension and switch from negative to positive thinking.

For psychological or physiological reasons, freezing may occur, similar to when a computer freezes—you press the keys, but nothing happens, the screen does not react to signals. The same thing happens to the brain when it is in a state of stagnant overtension. In this state, we say a person has become hung up. When this happens to a computer, it must be switched off and rebooted.

It is freezing of the brain's Discharge and Recharge mechanism that causes stress and its chronic development, neurotic disturbances, and psychosomatic illnesses.

The natural way to launch the brain's Discharge and Recharge mechanism is to reduce the high tension that has accumulated. It must be reduced to zero. This, in the same way as switching off a computer, will bring about Discharge.

Tension is reduced to zero during the transition between wakefulness and sleep, for example, and can occur spontaneously during therapeutic and health-improving exercises, such as yoga, psychoanalysis, therapy, and training sessions. Cross-country skiing, working out, listening to music, and so on can also promote this.

In some cases, reducing tension necessary for activating the Discharge and Recharge mechanism can occur by raising tension to a critical level as happens when the brain resorts to its defense reaction.

Example
A patient told about how she was under immense stress; her son had to go to court.

In the courtroom she was extremely nervous, she could not calm down or stop herself from shaking. She had trouble breathing, and her heart was thumping.

Then suddenly... her body began rhythmically swaying on its own, she immediately calmed down, and the situation stopped bothering her...

This adaptation mechanism associated with reflex elimination of stress-induced overtension is also known in another sphere of life, in cases of extreme physical loads that are naturally accompanied by nervous tension.

For example, a runner suddenly feels lighter after reaching a certain threshold of physical exertion. This phenomenon of tension elimination, feeling lighter, is usually called "getting your second wind."

In actual fact, second wind has nothing to do with, it is the logical result of reaching a state of mental and physical equilibrium.

This same feeling of lightness accompanied by a sense of soaring and weightlessness can also arise at the peak of profound relaxation, without any stress. This is what happens during meditation.

Release from tension and activation of the brain's Discharge and Recharge mechanism can also occur when drinking alcohol, which creates a temporary effect with a negative aftereffect.

Factors that remove tension can give rise to a new dependence.

In this sense, dependencies can be both beneficial and harmful, for example, creative pursuits or jogging can also become a dependency, as can the use of alcohol, tranquilizers, or going to see a psychologist.

In problematical cases, a doctor prescribes tranquilizers or antidepressants for removing stress and tension.

Now we better understand why they are used—to reduce tension, that is, to promote the creation of conditions in which the brain's evolutionary mechanism of self-control—Discharge and Recharge—is automatically activated.

The Key makes it possible to Discharge and Recharge any time you want.

How Does Discharge and Recharge Work?

Use of the Key techniques helps to reduce tension, remove stress, and switch to positive thinking very quickly.

I have determined that this mechanism is launched when a person finds the right rhythm, when running, swimming, and so on. Discharge occurs, whereby you know the zero point has been reached when your movements become automatic and your head becomes empty, i.e. you have reached a state of inner freedom.

A marathon trainer I know once said to me: the main thing is to find the running pace!

This means finding the right rhythm of movement.

Therefore, you can acquire the same effect of Discharge and Recharge without running or swimming, providing you find an automatic rhythm in whatever movement you are performing.

If, right where you are, you swing your arms effortlessly back and forth, twist, or choose another repetitive movement that feels comfortable, you will experience Discharge. While doing this, it is important to let your thoughts run free, in other words, just think about whatever comes to mind. You will be able to Discharge faster if you speed up your movements whenever distressing emotions surface.

Many of the existing methods use a similar exercise.

But I am the first person to describe in scientific and practical terms the criteria with the help of which you can quickly and easily obtain a high and guaranteed effect from this exercise.

> **The criterion for achieving Discharge is Zero—a neutral state characterized by emotional distancing, that feeling of not caring less about things that used to bother you, or even a feeling of emptiness in your head.**
>
> **This phenomenon is accompanied by automatic movements.**

The discharging mechanism, which activates a transfer from minus to plus, must pass through Zero—a brief state when your head is empty and you could not care less about anything.

Depending on your initial state, on how high your initial tension is, on whether you have had enough sleep, or on how much negativity you have built up, a range of different characteristic phenomena may arise—intensified unpleasant emotions, a feeling of deep peace, extraordinary lightness, sleepiness, or a catharsis (tears or laughter, spontaneous body movements).

When you reach the Zero state, your problems lose their immediacy, you look at them impartially.

If you ask anyone, when and under what circumstances they experienced similar feelings, they will most often say that it was while on vacation at a health resort, or on a trip far from home, when any problems became less immediate and could be viewed in a detached way.

And in that Zero state during Discharge something amazing happens!

Without any effort, in a very natural way, you suddenly notice that you are thinking about something positive!

Recharge has occurred.

From this point on, pleasant episodes, childhood memories, for example, begin coming to mind naturally, future plans materialize, and positive thinking is activated.

This exercise takes different lengths of time depending on the person—one may need five minutes, while another requires thirty to reach the Zero state.

But the result is always equally positive. Different people express how they feel in the same way, "I feel so much better!" and "Now I know what I want and what to do!"

This is passive recharge, when the brain undergoes positive recharge itself in conditions where the mechanisms of natural self-control are released in a Zero state from the blocks aroused by stress.

Example after a terrorist act—a bomb blast during a street parade in Kaspiisk, Daghestan, the Northern Caucasus
An injured 14-year-old boy lies in a hospital ward after undergoing emergency surgery; three shards were removed from his neck. There is still one more to be removed and

the surgeons are discussing the prospects for another operation.

The boy has been unable to sleep for three days, he dozes in fits and starts, and cannot relax. Whenever he closes his eyes, he sees the explosion replayed in his mind's eye.

He is reluctant to talk. This makes it impossible to begin effective verbal psychotherapy. The Key was used: the boy was asked to hold his left arm out in front of him (his right arm was in a cast) and imagine it moving to the left and then to the right by itself.

The motor reflex was activated—his arm began moving.

This guided ideomotor technique was repeated five times; the procedure lasted for about two minutes. The boy was tired, he lowered his arm. And the muscles of his face relaxed for the first time, his face became more symmetrical. He closed his eyes and sighed, and when he opened them again a few minutes later, his expression was more candid, his eyes brighter.

Approximately 10 minutes after the procedure, he began talking without any prompting and asked why his arm had moved by itself.

Verbal psychotherapy could begin. That day he fell asleep peacefully for the first time.

Active Recharge

When practicing active recharge you think, after beginning discharge, about the feeling of wellbeing you want to reach in the future.

And when distressing emotions arise or you feel a lack of confidence in yourself, you "pulverize" these psychological traumas and psychological barriers by speeding up your movements.

As your tension decreases and you are released from the negative emotions that have accumulated, you can create new desirable habits, attitudes, and ways of behavior in this space that has been freed up in your mind, as though turning over a new leaf, in so doing attuning your body to improve your health and discover and develop desirable qualities and capabilities.

By learning how to Discharge and Recharge and attuning yourself to feel alert and successfully resolve your problems, you can quickly expand and develop your creative and volitional capabilities, and learn how to manage those processes you were previously unable to control.

After Discharge and Recharge, it is recommended you do the Aftereffect Stage. The Moment of Truth you became acquainted with in the Key Stress Test.

This brings about intensive rehabilitation.

Before very long, you will reap the benefits of the same positive therapeutic effect you would acquire after a long vacation.

Since training in the Key Method more often that not begins in a state of stress-induced overtension, you must first undergo Discharge, as in the following examples.

You can do this Discharge and Recharge in any very problematical situation you may find yourself to intensify the effect of the brief self-control techniques and the regular five-minute Synchrogymnastics aimed at maintaining equilibrium.

All the Answers are Within You

She came a long way from another city to my Stress Management Center.

I asked her why she had come to see me.

I asked what she expected, what result she wanted to take back home with her.

She said that her grandchildren were all grown, so she no longer needed to spend so much time caring for her children and was looking for something for herself.

She complained that she changed her job every three years and could not bring anything to its logical conclusion. Now she recognized her own character traits in her granddaughter and this greatly concerned her.

She hoped that with the help of the Key she would come to understand her mission in life.

This question very much concerned her because she always did everything she set her mind to with satisfaction and good results.

*For example, she had worked for the past three years
as chief accountant in an institution and had assimilated
that profession so well that now she could see accounting
in its entirety, as a holographic image, a single whole.
She saw the ways in and ways out of this system, saw
where there was debit, and where credit, what should be
added, and what taken away, how to shift things around
to achieve the most profit, how to reach a balance. She
gave her friends advice about how to work more efficiently
and was surprised that they could not see for themselves
the solutions to many situations that she understood
straightaway.*

*But despite all of this she complained that she
had failed to accomplish anything in her life. So now
she wanted to change her profession and do something
different, but she did not know what.*

*"That's why I have come to see you," she said when
she had finished telling me her story.*

*"Perhaps you are just tired of your job and what to
do something new?"*

"No, I like my job!"

*"So what do you want to accomplish? Are you trying
to say that if you are an accountant, for instance, you
want to move up the career ladder until you become the
minister of finance? Then you die and you'll be buried
with dignity. But how is this more interesting than dying
as an accountant? That was not what you wanted to
accomplish, was it?*

"So what is accomplishment then?"

*"Doing what you like best. Doing something that brings
you satisfaction, as well as a feeling of accomplishment.
The formula of happiness is amazingly simple: doing what
you like best and also getting paid for it. There you have
complete balance between your spiritual and material
requirements."*

*"The problem is that I can do anything with
satisfaction!"*

*"Your true mission is something you cannot live
without. And, as you grow in what you do, you do it*

better than anyone else. For example, in Karma Yoga, one of the questions asked is: who is higher, a king or a shoemaker? And the answer is: he is higher who does his job better. Then he is not only of use to himself, but also to other people. This creates a harmonious exchange between man and society.

"And I too have created a similar aphorism," I told her proudly, "Find something only you can do, and you will be indispensable."

"Will I be able to find the answers with the help of your Key?"

"Yes, when you immersed yourself in your job as an accountant," I replied, "you understood it so well that you began to see all the details from a distance, as an integrated system. But life is even bigger than this accounting, and in order to be able to see it as an integrated whole, you have to distance yourself even more. As the saying goes, you can only see the big picture from a distance."

"But what do you mean, distance yourself even more?"

"You need to distance yourself emotionally."

"That is something I have never been able to do, I am forever churning thoughts over in my head." "Are you sure you can never free yourself from your chaotic thoughts?"

"Yes! Even on vacation or when traveling, I always seem to be working, I can never unwind!"

I asked her to stand up and try the Rocking technique for five minutes.

She tried to let her body sway, like a tree in the wind, and said that swaying did not suit her, it irritated her.

"Try folding your arms across your chest as naturally as you can and imagine you are standing in a train carriage and the train is moving and rocking you.

"Perhaps that is better for you?" I asked her.

She said she did not find that comfortable either.

So then I suggested she try the Twisting technique.

After a few minutes of doing these movements, she began complaining of pain in her side. I suggested she try

*the Cross-Country Skier technique. And I showed her
how to do it.*

She said she had never skied before.

*I explained that it was entirely irrelevant whether
or not she had ever skied, the main thing was to choose
some movement that she could do easily, that she could
keep up effortlessly.*

*I warned her that Discharge had several particular
requirements: she must allow her thoughts to run at
random, that is, not drive out any unpleasant thoughts,
but, on the contrary, allow thoughts to come at will. I
explained to her that this was precisely what the discharge
process was all about, allowing thoughts to flow freely
while repeating the same movements.*

*I explained to her that while she performed the
exercises, she should not try to hold back any emotions that
may arise, for example, she may feel sleepy or experience
a feeling of joy, she may feel teary, or experience a feeling
of lightness, or she may even feel temporary depression;
she should just let it all come.*

*"Let come what comes!" I said. "This is the gist of
discharge, while repeating the same movements, you
allow everything the nervous system requires to flow
through you. And your reward will be clear sailing!"*

*"But," I warned her, "you need to reach a zero
state."*

*"But what does that mean, zero state?" she
questioned.*

*"A person cannot jump from minus to plus. This
means that to reach a plus state, that is, to put yourself
in a good mood with positive thoughts, you have to pass
through zero. It is like a car's gearbox, where you can only
switch gears by going through the neutral position, when
all systems are unlocked. Some people are quick to pass
through the zero state, while others take longer, there are
many reasons for this—the level of tension, whether the
person is sick or not, and so on."*

People instinctively look for conditions or some movement that can reduce tension and activate this discharge-recharge mechanism in their body.

They may even try to achieve this by drinking alcohol, taking anti-depressants, going on trips, working out at the gym, or jogging.

There are cases when a person is unable to carry out discharge and recharge for different reasons because the tension does not decrease to the necessary zero level, and then psychosomatic illnesses appear.

These illnesses can be successfully cured if conditions are created for discharge and recharge. Nature itself restores and returns everything to normal.

"The main thing," I told her, "is to create these zero conditions in the brain, then you can discharge the old accumulated negative processes and recharge to new positive life prospects."

"But how will I know when I have reached zero in this exercise?"

"I will tell you the secrets of self-control which are not written in any book in the world: there are two criteria of this zero state: when your movements become automatic and you can perform them effortlessly, and when your head becomes empty."

"This is when you feel as though you don't care about a thing. You feel total indifference; when your thoughts and emotions seem to be separate from each other. This phenomenon is called emotional distancing.

"In actual fact, it is a state of inner harmony.

"When there is harmony, there are no thoughts, because thinking is what establishes new relations for resolving some conflict by creating a place for these new relations in the existing picture of the world.

"Discharge leads to full coordination of the internal systems, to harmony, and if there are no problems, there is no thinking required to resolve them.

"Start doing the exercise!" I suggested. "Just do whatever movements you feel comfortable with and while you do so, let your thoughts flow. When the wave of *tension seems to grow at times, or particularly unpleasant thoughts arise, speed your movements up. You will notice that very soon this work becomes so easy that you won't want to stop! This is what we want—this means you have discharged completely and reached Zero. Then I will tell you what to do next. And today you will have a wonderful evening!"*

After saying all that, I left to get on with my own business, returning from time to time to keep an eye on the process.

Ten minutes later, she said she had changed the initial movements, had found more comfortable movements. Now this exercise had become easier for her.

Twenty minutes later, she was still doing the exercise, but when I asked what she was thinking about, she replied that many thoughts were will buzzing around in her head.

Twenty-five minutes later, she said that she did not want to think about anything, she could not be bothered concentrating on any thoughts, she could not care less about anything now.

She said the movements seemed to be happening of their own accord, that now she could keep on doing them all night if she had to.

At this point, I asked her to sit down and do what is called the Aftereffect Stage. The Moment of Truth.

"Sit comfortably," I said, "look in front of you at nothing in particular, keep your eyes unfocused, like when you are tired or far away in thought. You don't have to relax. Just sit passively, resting. Let your thoughts run as they will, just let thoughts come randomly into your head, don't do anything to hinder the process. No matter what thoughts arise, it is all for your good. These are precisely the conditions in which you will feel release.

"This is the secret of self-control: people usually put up resistance to bad thoughts, but you need to let them come. Let them flow as they will. But in the conditions of psychophysiological protection, in the conditions of the Key!

"And you will obtain a wonderful result!"

"How long do I have to sit like this?" she asked.

"As long as your body needs, as long as it wants to sit. When the restoration process ends, you will feel yourself that you have had enough, that you want to move. Until then, just sit as long as you want to. If you want, you can close your eyes, if you don't want to, sit with your eyes open, but do not close your eyes on purpose before you need to, let it all come naturally, let everything happen as it will."

A few minutes later, her eyes closed and a beatific smile appeared on her face. When I asked what she was thinking about now, she said she was not thinking about anything.

"My head is empty, I don't want to think about anything!"

"When have you felt like this before? A year ago, ten years ago?"

"I don't think I have every felt it!"

"And how can you describe briefly how you feel?"

"I feel a sense of peace, a feeling of goodwill and wellbeing."

"Sit like that, please, as long as you want, and then when you feel fresher, stand up yourself. Now the cherished process of rehabilitation, restoration, is going on inside you. In this way, you can restore your health in the shortest time, the same as if you had spent two months at a health resort! Rest!"

She rested in this Aftereffect Stage for 15 minutes. Then she opened her eyes and said that her vision had improved, she could see objects clearer and more precisely, they were more vibrant.

"Yes," I said, "your eyes have become clearer, and your head has most likely become clearer too."

Suddenly she stood up and walked around the room as though she was listening to something.

"What's the matter?" I asked.

"I am amazed," she replied, "the noise in my head has gone, there's no noise."

"What noise?"

"For four years, I have had this constant noise in my head, sometimes louder, sometimes quieter, but constant, all the time. It bothers me. Now for some reason the noise has gone."

"If the noise has gone, it means it was vascular noise. I am a doctor and I can tell you that the noise was due to being in a state of constant tension. You need to repeat this exercise for 3-4 weeks once a week, and also perform five techniques for one minute every day. In this five-minute Synchrogymnastics, the first techniques are designed to open up the neck and chest section of the spine. They help to cure osteochondritis and streamline the work of the cerebral vessels, then the noise will stop entirely.

"And now tell me how you feel, what is going on with you now?"

"I feel good! I feel rested! I feel as though I have known you and your Center and this room for at least ten years, although I came to see you just one hour ago. That's interesting. I can probably adapt to other conditions faster with the help of your exercises. When I go on another business trip to a new city, I'll try it!"

"What else? What do you feel?"

"You know, I have calmed down. I realize I've never had the time to think calmly about myself and my life. Now I realize it was pointless to worry, my life has not been meaningless. I have raised my children, my grandchildren, I've always had an interesting job, so everything's worked out for me!"

"And did you really not know that? You told me yourself about your children and grandchildren and your interesting job!"

"Yes, I knew, but only in theory, in my mind, and now I have found reconciliation with myself, I have calmed down."

Automatic Psychoanalysis

Once I was invited to the home of some relatives I had not seen for ten years.

It was a rare occasion.

It turned out my help as a doctor was required.

The wife had been experiencing erratic jumps in blood pressure and glucose level for the second week in a row. She had never had anything like this before. Three times in the past two weeks this healthy energetic woman had had to call the ambulance. She was not going to work and, in a panic, had asked the advice of doctors, but the reason for the abrupt decline in her health remained a mystery.

"I don't understand what's the matter, I don't know what's going on. You know, I am a doctor myself and have consulted with other doctors, we only use medication to bring down blood pressure and sugar content, but I can't sleep at night and I roam all day around the apartment, I can't calm down. And there is no reason! On the contrary, we are celebrating, my daughter's just given birth to a baby girl, I should be happy. But for some reason I am in a panic!"

"Stand up, please, try holding your arms stretched out in front of you, relax them. Don't rush! Imagine them smoothly moving apart in opposite directions, as though they are being pulled by some force. You can't? You can't get in the mood? Then try something else. Move them apart and then imagine they are being pulled toward each other like magnets."

"Why are you making me do these stupid movements? I can't concentrate, I am anxious."

"What are you thinking about?"

"I don't know, I just don't feel good. As though something unpleasant is going to happen."

"But can you tell me something specific about what is troubling you?"

"I am thinking about why I suddenly have this illness, after all, I am a healthy woman, I have always had things to keep me busy, I have never been sick, and

now everything is going wrong, and they're expecting me at work. But I can't go to work and that is making me worry even more!"

"Okay, if it is difficult for you to hold you arms before you in a relaxed way and distract yourself from your unpleasant thoughts, try crossing them over your chest and just sway, as though you were riding in a train. Imagine you are standing and the train is moving and rocking you. Rock mechanically back and forth. And let your thoughts come as they will."

"I can't relax!"

"You don't need to relax. I am only asking you to sway back and forth any way you like and just let your thoughts flow."

"But I can't relax when I am thinking bad thoughts! And I can't get rid of them."

"Please, you don't have to get rid of any thoughts. Just sway, you don't have to do anything else. Just rock back and forth. You can think about what you want, because it is not important what you are thinking about, it is important just to sway. It is even good that you are thinking unpleasant thoughts while you are swaying."

"Why? I should be thinking about good things, but I can't!"

"The more you think about bad things while you are rocking your body, they more you will be released from them. And then you can think about good things."

"And how long do I have to rock like this? Won't I fall? I already feel dizzy."

"No one ever falls. Spread your feet wider if you are afraid. And you will stop feeling dizzy in about 2-3 minutes. This exercise helps to cure dizziness and motion sickness. I do it for pilots and astronauts who train in a centrifuge. I'll tell you about it later. You just keep swaying!"

"You don't say? I didn't know that you can cure motion sickness by rocking."

"That is precisely how it is cured, because you give your vessels a chance to train. While before,

every time you felt yourself getting dizzy, you were afraid and wouldn't allow yourself to train. But you need to do it under the supervision of a specialist."

"How long to I have to rock like this? I'm tired already."

"Every minute it will get easier. Choose the rhythm and form of movement that are most comfortable for you so that you can sway longer. Try swaying, for example, in a circle, or do other repetitive movements that are easier for you, it is supposed to be pleasant."

"How long have I been swaying?"

"Ten minutes."

"How much longer?"

"Now try spreading your arms again, hold them in front of you in a relaxed way and imagine they are smoothly moving in opposite direction. You smiled? Why?"

"Yes, they are moving apart! I didn't expect it! But why?"

"Because your tension has been reduced. Keep on rocking some more!"

"I'm tired of it! I want to sit down or lie down. I feel so sleepy all of a sudden."

"Sit down and look in front of you, without looking at anything in particular. Keep your eyes unfocused, look vacantly, as though into a fog. Don't close your eyes straight away, only if you feel the need. I am telling you as a doctor, the end of the Discharge exercise is called the 'Aftereffect Stage. The Moment of Truth'."

"I am sitting, I don't want to talk. My head feels empty. Oh my goodness! I know why my blood pressure has been acting that way! I was waiting for a week for my daughter to have her baby, and now she's given birth, but the baby has not been taking the breast for a week, and no one knows why. So for two weeks I've been feeling this tension!"

"What? And you didn't know that?"

"Yes, I knew. But I just realized now, after my head became clear and free of all my troubling thoughts, that

this is precisely where all my worry has been coming from!"

"You see, psychoanalysis was successful, automatically!"

"But what should I do now? Wait! I just realized what I should do! I have to call a doctor I know, he's a good pediatrician, he will help me solve the baby's feeding problems. I forgot all about him in my worry!"

"You can call him later, but now lie down and rest!"

"You know, I often hear about people finding things, a key, for example, they have forgotten where they put in their hurry. And they find it precisely when they calm down, when their thoughts are freed from problems and commotion."

"The Key helps people to find a key? Yes, I need to rest, I have calmed down somewhat, I will sleep for a while and then I'll give that pediatrician a call."

The next day, she went back to work. Her blood pressure and sugar count were restored to normal after a good night's sleep without medication.

This is how the automatic psychoanalysis which legitimately occurred during Discharge brought about coordination of her mental and physiological processes, and integrity of "body and soul" was restored.

And "integrated" in many languages means "healthy."

The Key Anti-Stress Training

Psychological training in any activity is based on anti-stress training—preventive raising of resistance to stress that can be applied to future stressful situations.

The main problem of this kind of training is that people learn in one situation, while they have to use the knowledge and skills acquired in different, including emergency, situations. And if they are unable to overcome their fear, they could forget everything they have learned at the crucial moment.

The Key anti-stress training has convincingly confirmed its high effectiveness in a variety of different situations, such as preparing children to participate in an international music festival sponsored by the Vladimir Spivakov International Charity Foundation, as well as training the personnel who raised the *Kursk* nuclear submarine, military specialists sent to combat zones, rescue squads and other people involved in dangerous and stressful professions, test pilots in the international Mars-500 space program, and athletes, including the participants in world cups and Olympic Games.

Training test pilots of the Mars-500 International Space Program

Athletes learn Synchrogymnastics. The Olympic Games. China

The Key anti-stress training has also proved its benefit for future mothers and is readily used by them to cope with stress and ensure that pregnancy, childbirth, and, later, breastfeeding all go well. It is recommended that they begin the training during the first half of pregnancy.

Everyone knows how difficult it is to feel confident when you are faced with an important meeting. Your thoughts are often thrown off course, and you find yourself overcome by self-doubt and the doom and gloom of imminent failure.

In order to raise your self-confidence, you need to surmount that psychological barrier and wipe out all negative images of your potential lack of success.

You can perform the Key techniques and Synchrogymnastics exercises as a form of psychological training to induce mental simulation of the way you feel and imagine what you will do in the stressful situation you are about to face. And in particularly stressful cases, you can also add the Discharge and Recharge procedures.

For example, you are getting ready for an exam.

You want to have a clear head and confidence in yourself so that you can get a good grade and pass the exam with flying colors.

As you put yourself in the right mood, you think about how you want to feel as you are taking the exam. But fear that you will make a mistake, negative emotions, and stress make it difficult to create this mood.

With the help of the Slapping Your Back technique for example, you can begin thinking about the upcoming exam with increasing confidence. You might even try imagining that you are not going to take an exam, you are going to a party instead.

But you are unable to create this mood, you are too nervous.

This is when the Key techniques can help you to emotionally distance yourself.

Imagine the future exam situation.

In so doing, notice how your body is responding, for example, your muscles are tensing up, your heart is beating faster, and so on.

Remove the tension that arises using the Slapping Your Back technique or another exercise from Synchrogymnastics that suits you better.

When you reach a state of relaxation, imagine the future situation that is bothering you again.

In this way, by responding to your tension and removing it, you reach a state where visual simulation of the stress factor no longer arouses overtension in response.

By freeing yourself from undesirable reflex reactions, you are able to confidently think about the optimal mood you wish to be in during the upcoming exam.

The Key anti-stress training consists of two parts:
1. **Neutralizing the undesirable reflex reaction to a stress situation by visualizing the situation from the point of emotional distancing generated by the Key.**

2. **Forming a desirable reflex reaction to the stressful situation you are about to encounter by visualizing, with the help of the Key, the mood you wish to experience.**

If stress is very high and the method described above to remove it does not yield a rapid result, you can begin the Discharge procedure, trying to think of how you want to feel and what you want to do during the upcoming exam.

As Discharge occurs, tension decreases, your thoughts become calmer, and, now, as you approach Zero, you can think about how you want the future situation to take shape with confidence.

After passing through Zero (the neutral state), when your head is empty and free of thoughts, you will be able to confidently think in a natural way about successfully passing the exam.

You have overcome your mental block and you can confidently go and take the exam, you will successfully pass it.

So there are differences between Discharge and Recharge during rehabilitation after a stressful event and during anti-stress training before an upcoming stressful situation.

For example, in the examples I described earlier, Discharge and Recharge occurred after stressful situations where they released the accumulated tension and negative emotions and brought about a natural transfer to positive thinking spontaneously.

During anti-stress training before stressful situations, Discharge and Recharge are used to channel positive thoughts in a specific direction, for example, to prepare you for taking an exam, holding an important meeting or talks, participating in a competition.

Your ability to manage your wellbeing decreases if your emotions are fed by the body's vegetative reactions. For example, if fear is accompanied by pounding of the heart, headaches, or heaviness or sluggishness in the arms and legs, this increases fear.

In order to break out of this vicious circle when learning self-control skills, the Key techniques can be combined at the initial stage with recommended medical methods for correcting vegetative disturbances, for example, acupuncture, reflexology, and so on.

Slapping Your Back for stutterers—the main exercise for loosening up and releasing tension

How Anna Took Her Exams

Anna came with her mother. She was to take some exams to enroll in music school. Anna is a very talented young girl. At the age of 15, she had already independently made a four-minute musical cartoon. But the thought of how she will reach for the handle of the door behind which sits the high examination commission is making her shake in fear.

"Such important professors are waiting for me!" says Anna, "I am afraid."

She is so nervous, she has been unable to sleep for the past three nights. And she really wants to get into the school, it is her dream. Naturally her mother is also losing sleep.

"Stand up please," I said to her, "close your eyes, and imagine that you are reaching out for that very door handle and opening the door. How do you feel? Describe your sensations."

"My legs are trembling, and it is difficult for me to breathe."

"Now think about how you will pass the exam well, that you will act confidently."

"I can't think of anything like that, I am afraid, I can't think positively, I will certainly fail the exam!"

"Now imagine that your arms are rising up, they are light, like balls of fluff."

"I can't!"

"Then shake your arms as though you are about to dive into the water, limber up as you would before a competition."

"By why, I'm not taking part in a competition? I'm thinking about the exam!"

"That does not matter. Even weight-lifters and chess players need to limber up. You need to remove the tension. Shake yourself a little, as though you are at a discotheque, since you have the jitters anyway!"

"I'm shaking. It's not making any difference, I'm still afraid.

"Shake, shake, find a rhythm that you enjoy shaking to. Try to speed it up or slow it down, and you will find the right rhythm for yourself, one you want to keep on doing, as though you are riding a horse."

"Yes, that's right, like on a horse!"

"And think about how you are confidently walking into the exam room."

"I cannot think about that, I'm still afraid."

"Then sway back and forth, sway, sway, wriggle and roll. Keep it up for as long as you can, don't rush. Then

everything will be fine and you will pass the exam with flying colors!"

Ten minutes later, I asked Anna, "How are you doing?"

"I feel calmer."

"Can you think now about how you will confidently walk into the exam room?"

"Yes."

"Well, think about it."

"I am thinking."

"And whenever any inner tension surfaces, shake yourself again, sway, or wave your arms, remove the tension by limbering up, and think again."

"I should do this limbering up every time I find a hurdle blocking my way to my dreams?"

"Yes, climb over it just as though it were a hurdle!"

Twenty minutes later I asked Anna, "How are you doing?"

"Fine!"

"Now imagine your arms are rising up, they are light, like balls of fluff."

"O! They're rising up! All by themselves. How is that?"

"And now imagine that your arms are wings that are carrying you high above the clouds to meet the warm sun. And as you do this, imagine you are going to take your exam, with a light, joyous step, a clear head, and confidence in yourself. And everything will work out just fine."

"It's working! I'm not afraid!"

"Fly like that for a few minutes, then sit down and rest, you will have no trouble passing the exam."

When she left to go home, I gave Anna an assignment: to repeat the exercise herself before she went to bed, and before the exam, as she went into the room, to limber up in her mind.

Anna passed with flying colors, she got an A.

But two days later, her mother phoned me and told me that Anna was getting nervous again before another exam. She could not sleep, and the exercise was not helping her. However, the mother herself was benefiting from it. She had become calmer and asked what techniques she could add.

When we met, Anna was again worked up and could not release her tension herself.

So I asked her to sit on a chair and checked her neck muscles with my fingers.

They were as hard as a brick.

I gently massaged her neck.

After that, she was able to perform the techniques effectively.

I taught the mother how to do the massage if the situation should repeat itself.

Anna passed the exams brilliantly. She was the youngest student to get the highest marks at the school's entrance exams that year.

Nadezhda shares her experience.

"People were getting laid off at work, and on Monday I was supposed to give a report at a meeting which would decide both my own fate and the fate of the other people I worked with.

"I was so worried about this report that I could not concentrate and lost a lot of sleep.

"And this is what I did.

"At a convenient moment, when no one was around, I did the Key techniques.

"My tension quickly fell away, and my body began swaying in a pleasant rhythm as though being buffeted by waves or like a tree in the wind.

"While swaying like this, I began to feel my thoughts calming down, I began imagining and saying to myself: 'I am healthy, I am full of energy, I will give a wonderful report, the more stress I feel, the stronger I become, and at the critical moment I will find the best solution, and everything will be fine!'

"I did this for three evenings, 15 minutes at a time. Then I sat down for about five minutes and simply rested, waiting for my head to clear and a new surge of energy to appear, as I had been taught.

"Three days later, I gave a wonderful report!

"And while I was doing these techniques, I also thought, 'I cannot stand sweets!' I let these thoughts come unhindered.

"And for two weeks my craving for sweets disappeared. Now I have to repeat the procedure again."

Two weeks later, Nadezhda talked about how natural she feels in this state of being she has discovered in herself. She feels outgoing and uninhibited, free to be herself.

"By discovering this, I have discovered my true essence," she said, "which lies at some deep level within me, I feel. And the same is true for everyone.

"Since I began using the Key techniques," said Nadezhda, "I have become less hung up on my complexes, I have begun to better understand myself and others, I feel less inhibited when socializing with colleagues at work, and I can tackle any new task with greater confidence."

Chapter 6.
How to Choose the Key to Yourself

> *Today you are in for a wonderful evening!*
> *You probably studied well in school!*
> *How your eyes shine! Fabulous!*
> *You probably have some secret, right?*
> *You want me to tell you something?*
> *Stretch out your hand!*
> *Today you are in for a wonderful evening!*
>
> Hasai Aliev

The Star of Self-Control

The Star of Self-Control, so called for its multifaceted diversity like the many sides of a star, is a set of exercises that is designed to help you choose the Key to yourself. These exercises should preferably be performed for the first five days every day or every other day. Do them once a day whenever it is convenient for you; they take about 30 minutes.

After you become familiar with them, you can use the exercises separately for different purposes, along with the regular five-minute Synchrogymnastics, which allow you to maintain a high level of creative and physical efficiency in any circumstances. There may be times, however, particularly if an acute problem has arisen in your life, when you will want to perform the entire set of exercises.

First do the Key Stress Test to gage the level of your tension. If you are in for a busy week involving some challenging task, or you have just quit smoking, or you are about to go on a demanding business trip, and your tension has abruptly risen, your arms will remain immobile despite your every wish to have them levitate spontaneously.

You can remove this extra tension with the help of the tension-releasing Slapping Your Back exercise, then check your level of tension again by means of the Test.

If the Slapping exercise is not enough to restore your inner balance, you can also do some of the other tension-releasing techniques. For example, you could do the Twisting exercise until you achieve complete Discharge and Recharge (see Chapter 8 for a full description of these exercises).

Soon you will begin to feel for yourself which techniques help you best in particular situations.

You will be amazed! From the very first day, practicing the Key Method will help you to feel calmer and find effective solutions more easily in those same stressful situations that used to confound you.

Every Endeavor Is Rewarded by a Payoff

> *Positive thinking means focusing on the payoff and not becoming hung up on failure.*
>
> Hasai Aliev

The brain's mechanisms are structured so that when your endeavors are rewarded with the desired payoff, tension decreases and energy is generated to continue your endeavor.

If there is no payoff, energy is not liberated but spent instead on trying to find out where you went wrong and correcting it.

This feedback system is conducive to choosing effective ways to manage your life and endeavors.

If your endeavors are continuously rewarded with the desired payoff, a burst of energy is released in the brain.

Endorphin-like substances are released into the blood. Success makes you feel as though you have grown wings!

The sky's the limit!

The shorter the time between the effort exerted and the desired outcome, the greater the pleasure you derive from the activity. So people try to find an activity they have a talent for, since this requires the least effort to achieve the best results.

This may seem funny, but it is true: scratching an itch is always so gratifying because the effort of scratching produces an instantaneous result.

The feeling of pleasant relief and satisfaction that arises when your endeavors yield the anticipated results is mental relaxation in concentrated form, or that state of free consciousness with which nature rewards you for a task well done.

Artificially inducing this state, by means of alcohol for example, disrupts natural development.

The Key Method helps to boost confidence in yourself and so achieve success.

A feeling of success is induced by choosing a technique that immediately yields the desired result. And if one technique produces no result, you simply ignore it and try another. In this way, the brain receives intensive positive impulses in a short time that are empowered by the payoff.

The sky's the limit!

The Key Guarantees a Payoff

A payoff is guaranteed, because if one technique
does not work, you choose another,
and you know how.

Hasai Aliev

At one time, eminent psychotherapist Milton Erickson used arm levitation to deepen hypnosis.

It is not actually important what you induce, a feeling of warmth in your arms or goose bumps over your body, or keeping your arm immobile or making it rise up in the air.

What is important is obtaining the desired result, then a so-called dominant focus, i.e. sustained focus of increased excitability in the cortex of the brain, is formed which makes it possible for you to control your inner state.

Of course, arm levitation was a familiar phenomenon even before Erickson's research, but he was the one to most convincingly verify this phenomenon in psychotherapy.

But what did Erickson and his followers do in cases when the arm did not levitate?

They intensified the suggestion by means of repetition or looked for another body reflex that was easier to induce.

In real practice, it is often difficult to achieve this levitation. There are people who, owing to their individual makeup, can do this immediately, while there are others who find it more difficult and take longer to accomplish it.

In order to raise the efficiency of the reflex being controlled in neurolinguistic programming (NLP) based on a study of Erickson's experience, an entire system has been created for choosing the means of communication that best suits the patient: visual, auditory, or kinesthetic.

Instead of this, however, I was able to find an essentially different solution that yields an almost instantaneous result and allows you to manage your inner wellbeing in the way you find easiest.

Here are two appealing tips:

1. If one technique does not work, abandon it and try another!

This is a simple, pleasant, and easy principle—do only what works!

As a result, when you do only what works, abandoning what does not work, tension is released and exercises that did not at first work for you begin to work.

2. Or…ATTENTION! You simply unwind, your tension disappears, and everything begins to work!

This is accomplished with the help of the Star of Self-Control, trying the ideomotor techniques and additional tension-releasing exercises, for example, the Synchrogymnastics, in turn until you find the one that works best for you.

Before and After the Key Techniques – The Key Stress Scale

Everyone knows what it is like to have a toothache, you can think of nothing else, but as soon as it goes away, you forget all about the pain you suffered.

In the same way, you soon forget the stress you were under as soon as it has been removed. You are busy with other tasks, you have returned to your normal state of wellbeing.

The psychological Key Stress Scale is used to assess the dynamics of your current state using the Key Method along with the psychophysiological Key Stress Test that shows whether you are tense or relaxed.

Before you begin, you are advised to assess your wellbeing at the moment, here and now, according to a 10-point scale, where 0 is calm, a feeling of complete peace, serenity, impartiality, and 10 is stormy, a feeling of maximum tension and discomfort. Consequently, your comfort level is also evaluated according to a 10-point scale, where 10 is maximum comfort, even euphoria. This subjective self-appraisal of your current state of wellbeing at the beginning and the end of the exercise makes it possible to define the dynamics of the result obtained from performing the techniques.

Technique for Rapidly Removing Stress

A young man came to see me in the hopes of finding a way to remove his stress.

"I assure you that our method works very quickly! What would you like to accomplish?"

"I would like to have my stress removed right now and then learn how to do it myself in the future."

"So you want to calm down, reach a state of equilibrium and boost your confidence? How long would you like this to take?"

"Fifteen minutes."

"I will make a note of your assignment—remove stress in fifteen minutes. And now assess your initial state according to the Key Stress Scale from 0 to 10. Ten is stormy, and zero is calm. What do you rate it at now?"

"8, I am very nervous."

"Stand up please. Note the noises all around you, telephones are ringing, you are standing and worrying. I suggest you calm down, remove your tension. You can't? Try holding your arms out in front of you and imagine they are automatically moving in opposite directions by themselves. Or try allowing them to levitate. Don't be surprised, these are reflexive movements that occur in response to the image you conjure up in your mind. These movements are called Key techniques, you need to choose the one that suits you. So the program is called 'Choosing the Key to Yourself.' Now sit down and rest quietly for another minute. What are you thinking about?"

"I'm not thinking about anything! All my worrying thoughts have disappeared. I feel relief, as though a weight has fallen from my shoulders. I wish it were always this way."

"This phenomenon is called 'empty mind.' Think back to the Key Stress Scale. How would you rate your inner state now?"

"I'm off the scale, I am even below zero, I feel very good. I can't remember when I felt so rested. Perhaps five years ago when I spent time out in the woods during my summer vacation."

"Now you can remove stress without going to the woods, without waiting for your vacation, at any time you want. Let's take a look at your assignment. You came to see me to learn how to remove your stress and wanted to do this in fifteen minutes. And you got what you wanted. See, you even removed your stress much faster, in just five minutes."

I see people going from minus to plus through zero every day.

Someone may say, for example: "I can't think about anything positive! All my thoughts are negative."

And then, as Discharge occurs, they say: "I am no longer thinking about anything. I feel indifferent to everything." And after this positive thoughts appear!

However, the reverse can also happen. Here is an example of passing from plus to minus. It turns out that this legitimately occurs through the zero state too.

A woman told me that she was reluctant to practice the Key Method because for three days she had been soaring in a euphoric state and wanted to sing and dance.

"And now," she said, "I feel deflated, tired, and devastated."

I asked:

"Does this happen to you often?"

"That's the problem, I am constantly either in seventh heaven or crashing back down to earth."

I suggested that whenever she experienced this slump, she should use the Key not to evoke a state of euphoria again but simply to restore her balance.

"Go ahead and allow yourself to fully feel your plunging spirits," I said, "then simply rest quietly in them, waiting for your mood to lift again."

This is what she did and 15 minutes later she felt restored.

> *"Now I have found a way to maintain equilibrium in my life," she said, her face alight with joy. "I won't allow myself to have sudden bouts of euphoria and will control my slumps, now I know how to restore my balance!"*

If we look at a graph, the distance between minus and plus is very short, but it is not so easy to actually cover this distance in practice. It requires Discharge and Recharge.

This is legitimate, euphoria, an energy-expending state, leads to exhaustion.

Whereas in a state of exhaustion, there is naturally no reaction at all—the brain is accumulating energy.

These practical examples prove my theory that there is a neutral state in the work of the brain, a place where the brain switches gears and undergoes restoration. You will find out about this in the chapter called "A New Model of Brainwork."

Just recently I had two patients who, following emotional upsets, always experienced empty minds and felt indifferent to everything. They act normally, understand everything, but are unable to concentrate. They take the medication prescribed by a neuropathologist and psychiatrist recommended for treating psychic traumas and brain disorders, but they do not feel any relief, rather they complain that they are in a kind of vacuum. In my terminology, they are caught in the neutral, zero state.

As I understand it, they have been unable to leave the neutral state because they did not undergo the correct restorative treatment. They have not been rehabilitated, but continue to work and lead an active lifestyle even though they always feel exhausted.

Evidently, many aspects of psychotherapy should be revised in the light of this new understanding about how the brain works.

On Training Conditions and Body Positions

In order to raise resistance to stress, training skills should be taught in conditions close to reality.

Extraneous sounds and other disturbances make it easier to reinforce self-control skills which you will be able to use in different, including emergency, situations.

The techniques can be performed standing, sitting, or lying, but in the standing position you will have more alternatives when choosing the techniques.

If you perform the exercises while standing, you will immediately understand how effective they are, because you can reach a comfortable state (very deep relaxation) without needing to assume a comfortable position, lying down on a couch, for example.

While standing, you will clearly recognize signs of tension release— the desire to perform energetic movements that lead to relaxation, that is, automatic swaying of the body.

Inducing relaxation while standing is a very good exercise in self-control; you learn how to retain your balance and not fall while you relax.

Very many people cannot relax because they are afraid of falling and losing control. But as you practice these techniques you realize that you can become deeply relaxed and retain control at the same time.

The first time, in order to feel more confident, you can place your feet further apart.

In addition, if you suffer from dizziness, you can get rid of it by training with the Key in the standing position.

At first you will be afraid of feeling dizzy, but in a few minutes, this fear will disappear.

And then, after a few training sessions, you will realize that you do not feel dizzy any more.

And, finally, practice has confirmed the benefit of training in the standing position. For example, if you have not had enough sleep and begin to relax, you will become drowsy, which is easier to overcome if you are standing. Most people who train using other methods, for example, meditation, relaxation, autogenic training in a comfortable sitting or lying position, simply fall asleep in these conditions. This is a natural physiological reaction for people who have not had enough sleep, when they find themselves in a comfortable position, they relax and fall asleep. Whereas other patients cannot relax while in a comfortable sitting or lying position during meditation or autogenic training because they are tense.

People who are initially in a highly tense state will now understand from my explanations how beneficial it is to do the Key tension-releasing exercises before meditating, praying, undergoing psychoanalysis, psychotherapy, or relaxation. I am referring to the Synchrogymnastics or levitation techniques, for example, which remove tension in 30-40 seconds.

I would like to share some of my interesting observations.

Practice shows that those patients who achieve the desired state of mental relaxation in the sitting or lying position during autogenic training or meditation are capable of reaching this state even faster when they are not in a comfortable position, while standing, for example.

Bedridden patients can also perform the Key techniques by moving their fingers, feet, wrists, turning their head, or moving their eyeballs and eyelids.

The value and power of the Key techniques lie in the fact that they are equally effective for removing tension and evoking a manageable state regardless of whether you perform the reflex movement with your entire arm or with your little finger.

After developing the skills for managing your inner state, you can use them for other activities, while jogging, for instance, thus making this or any other activity easier.

The acquired skills can make any workout a pleasant undertaking and raise its effectiveness.

Use your new-found skills at work without stopping what you are doing.

Whenever you feel tired or anxious, just think back to how you did the Slapping Your Back exercise at home and the sense of inner freedom and feeling of liberation and harmony it evoked. Remember the feeling of clarity and self-confidence you felt during your training sessions with the Key, and your mood will improve.

The Language of Objectives

When you are told, "You should be more modest!" give yourself a pat on the back; it will mean your self-kudos are finally working!

Hasai Aliev

I am talking about this because many books recommend that people use certain visualizations or utter certain phrases to induce a certain state of mind. For example, in autogenic training it is customary to repeat self-commands, such as "I am calm, balanced, full of energy!"

Think about boxers or fighters who limber up before fights. As they limber up, they know why they are doing it. They understand that after working out they will feel more energetic, stronger, and more confident, and this is their inner incentive.

If you want, you can give yourself encouraging commands, like in autogenic training, which, if you say them while performing the Key techniques, will make them even more potent: "I am healthy!", "I am full of energy!", "I feel great!"

Pay yourself a compliment and feel a blissful and satisfied smile spreading across your face.

Such compliments remove the blocks created in childhood when you abounded in energy but were kept in check and told not to do that and not to do the next thing, "stop it!", and so on.

Praise yourself and give yourself a boost of confidence. Give yourself another compliment! You cannot be dependent on other people's opinions and compliments forever.

And also think back to the best feeling you have ever felt in your life and project that feeling onto a future situation you are preparing for. In just the same way, in keeping with your natural inner voice, without forcing yourself, you can formulate other objectives as well. Let your thoughts run free with great abandon! The Key techniques are mediators between the mind and the body and help your thoughts to materialize, bringing the mind into harmony with the soul and activating the body's resources in order to make your dreams come true.

The Seven Basic Key Techniques

The Star of Self-Control for choosing the Key to Yourself consists of seven basic Key levitation techniques and numerous additional techniques you create yourself on the basis of the Key principle.

1. Moving Your Arms Apart
2. Bringing Your Arms Together
3. Raising Your Arms or Levitation
4. Flying
5. Turning
6. Head Movements
7. Haji-Murat's Finger

and techniques you create yourself.

When performing these techniques, focus your attention more on the goals you want to achieve using this method and not on the movements themselves, since that interferes with the process.

The first day you should spend 1-3 minutes on each of the techniques. After this, you can perform them as needed and as you wish.

You should begin choosing the Key in the order in which the techniques are described in the Star of Self-Control.

Later, by changing their order, you can adapt them to your personal needs in the way that best suits you.

Remember that repeating a successful technique removes tension and then you will find it easier to use the other techniques.

The goal of this training is to ultimately minimize the amount of effort and techniques necessary to achieve a manageable state.

This is the Key.

Moving Your Arms Apart

You are already familiar with this technique from the Key Stress Test. But here you will be using it to achieve a manageable state of being.

You can do it with your eyes open or closed, whichever you find most comfortable. Do what is easiest.

Stretch your arms out in front of you and imagine they are moving in opposite directions. It will be easier to do the exercise if you can distance yourself and expel extraneous thoughts from your head. And indeed this is the technique that teaches you how to distance yourself by banishing intruding thoughts at the necessary moment. If you have been able to clear your head of superfluous thoughts, your arms will begin moving. And as your arms move, you will be drawn deeper into a state of relaxation.

The main thing is to find an image that helps to activate this desired reflex.

That is:

1) Concentrate on your arms moving in opposite directions without physical effort;

2) Find an image that helps your arms to move apart. You could imagine your arms are pushing apart from each other like unipolar magnets, for example;

3) You can shake them slightly at the same time in order to remove any tension that is interfering with their movement.

You already know from this book that this is an easy way to check how tense you are; if your arms remain immobile, it means you should first do a few of the tension-releasing exercises and then try this technique again. For instance, do the exercise called Slapping Your Back from the Synchrogymnastics. You will immediately feel more relaxed, and when you try moving your arms apart again, you will find that the technique has begun working.

If you are still unable to do it, however, leave it for while and go on to the second.

If you are able to do it, repeat it a few times, and then go on to the second.

Bringing Your Arms Together

Move your arms apart in the usual way and then make them effortlessly move back together again.

I hope you will find this movement easier.

If you are able to do this exercise, repeat it a few times. And then try doing the first exercise—moving your arms apart.

Sometimes while you are doing these movements, you will feel as though some force is pulling at your arms. Choose a convenient image. Imagine, for example, that they are magnets being attracted to each other.

Moving the arms apart and bringing them together should be repeated several times, thus achieving continuous movement. If your arms do not want to move, you can push them slightly, or smile. You will immediately see that a smile reduces tension and your arms will begin moving more easily.

Once you feel your tension dissipating and a pleasant sense of unruffled calm descending, stay with these feelings for a few minutes. This is very beneficial.

Raising Your Arms or Levitation

Your arms are hanging by your sides. You can keep your gaze fixed on them or close your eyes. Do whatever is easiest for you. But do not move your eyes around, otherwise you will lose your inner concentration.

While looking at your arms, imagine they are getting lighter and beginning to rise, levitating. When your arms begin to float up, a mass of new pleasant sensations arises. The first time, this feeling comes as such a surprise that you involuntarily smile.

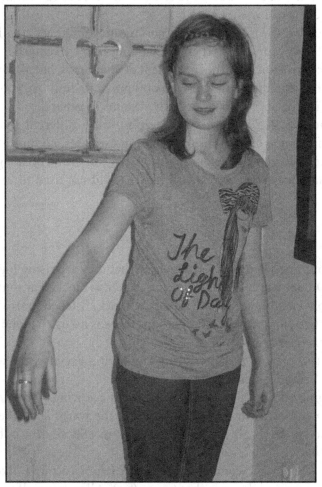

Alicia raising her arm

This works best immediately after doing the first two exercises, regardless of whether you were able to do them or not. And it is worth repeating them!

But now when you perform the techniques, imagine that when your arms are hanging they immediately begin levitating. But do not shake them, do not jiggle with them, let them levitate of their own accord.

This is a very pleasant and engaging technique. After you are able to do this, you will want to keep checking to see whether your arms rise up or not. It is like a children's game, like a new and entertaining toy. A toy for your health. You will want to do it at home, at work, while you're waiting for someone, or to remove stress. And as your arms start to levitate, make a wish…

Remember the thread of inner communication that arises between your will and your arms. Then, by tapping into this internal contact, you can control not only the movement of your arms, but also get rid of a headache, regulate your arterial blood pressure, improve your mood, and control the activity of your body systems in general.

If you are unable to do this exercise, try a different movement. After doing some of the tension-releasing exercises, go on to the next technique. And when you do something that works and do not get hung up on what does not work, the things that did not used to work start working.

Flying

When your arms begin to rise, imagine that they are rising higher and higher. Do not worry if this reflex movement is blocked at some point, it probably encountered a physiological block, osteochondrosis of the neck or chest, for example. But perhaps there is no osteochondrosis, so try this exercise again.

When the arms levitate during the Flying exercise, make things easier by bringing pleasant images to mind.

Imagine you are flying, that your arms are wings. You are flying high over the earth in a clear sky to meet the warm sun. There is an abundance of fresh air, it simply sparkles in effervescent bubbles all around you.

And wonder of wonders, your arms begin to move like wings themselves, up and down without any effort. Allow yourself to feel this state of flight. It is a wonderful feeling, we so often do not get enough of it here on earth. It is a state of freedom!

Help yourself to deepen this state by recalling similar feelings of flying in your sleep or other pleasant sensations associated with joy and inner freedom. If you want, remember a dance or a favorite song. Remember the best day in your life.

Flying

This is the Key's main exercise. It develops the experience of inner freedom. It is a feeling of harmony. It evokes an inflow of fresh energy and health.

The first time, this feeling may swamp you, it is euphoria! A celebration of the soul!

If, on the contrary, you want to cry, this means you are going through Discharge.

If you do not succeed in flying immediately, do not worry. You will soon find that you can.

Remember to look for the movements you find easiest to do. And when you repeat what works a few times, you will be able to do the exercises that did not work at first.

Repetition of the Key techniques evokes relaxation, and the body begins to sway. Sometimes your arms remain immobile, but your body has already begun swaying. Let your arms hang and sway on the waves of this Accommodating Biorhythm, like a child being pushed on a swing, like weeds floating in the water, like a flower bobbing in the wind ….

Now try the other exercises again, you will find you can do them.

Turning

The Turning exercise is very beneficial for your health, particularly for your spine, and it develops the ability, by means of small willful thrusts, to control the body.

Turning can be used separately or as a natural continuation of the levitation technique. Even if levitation did not work, you should definitely try the Turning exercise. You may find that it works very well for you, since you have less tension in your body.

Hold your arms out in opposite directions, just as you do in the Levitation technique when your arms float up. Now imagine that you and your arms begin to twist to the right, further and further. Your body become pliant like plasticine, because your muscles are relaxed and working effortlessly. Let this movement continue until you have turned as far as you can. Your head is at rest, while your muscles work as you turn. As you continue, your flexibility increases.

And now do the same thing in the other direction, to the left.

Head Movements

First version: sitting or standing, slowly turn your head in keeping with the Key ideomotor principle in search of a pleasant rhythm and pleasant pivotal points.

When you do this pleasant work, you are distracted from your problems and your nervous system calms down because while searching for pleasant sensations, as though anticipating a celebration, it becomes easier to breathe.

If you find a pleasant pivotal point where you want to leave your head, you should do this. This is because a pleasant pivotal point means you have reached the point of relaxation. That is, you have found a position to hold your head that sometimes involuntarily also occurs in everyday life when you are tired or when you are sitting deep in thought with your head tipped back slightly or to the side, or forward, whatever is more pleasant. This Key ideomotor movement is also sometimes activated spontaneously at the Aftereffect Stage after performing the Key techniques. This is a light healthy trance that you can freely control with minimum willful effort when you are attuned to improving your health.

Second version: sitting or standing, you initiate a light trance by turning your head, but very, very slowly, as slowly as possible, then even more slowly. This super slow movement is uncustomary, it requires your attention, so it quickly distracts you from your current problems and helps you to find the desired state of mental balance. The slower the movement, the faster the tension-releasing effect is activated.

If you are tired of looking for super slowness, take a rest. And it is now, when you are no longer doing anything and sitting, looking vacantly at nothing, that relaxation begins.

Third version: move your head by turning it from left to right or right to left, as you would do when showing disagreement, or up and down, as you do when you agree. The task is to choose a movement that you can continue as you wish without any effort, that is, an ideomotor movement.

It may also be easier to find your point of relaxation if you accompany vertical inclinations of the head, up and down, with vertical movements of the eyeballs, or horizontal turns, left and right, with horizontal movements of the eyeballs. Look for a very subtle, gentle movement. When you find it, you will immediately feel relief.

While doing this, your eyes can be closed or open, whichever you find more pleasant.

You can begin moving your head with moving your eyeballs. Or, if you find it more pleasant, you can limit yourself to just moving your eyes.

Interesting information about eye movement

There is a hypnotization method that uses the metronome. You sit and watch the needle of a metronome moving back and forth until you go into a trance. The effectiveness of this method depends, as we now understand from the Key principles set forth in this book, on the speed of the needle's movements back and forth, which should correspond to the person's current state. The higher the initial tension, the higher the initial speed.

The dance of a shaman who dances in a circle, moving to the left and then to the right, has a similar effect on the patient, in so doing possessing the patient's attention. He or she may say, "You don't have to believe me. I didn't believe it myself. But a shaman helped me. I just sat and did nothing, and my head stopped hurting." However, these people did not notice that while the shaman danced, their eyes were following him, moving rhythmically in a circle and back and forth.

This also explains people's taste in music—you choose the rhythm and volume that best reflects your inner state. Older people tend to enjoy the mellow tones of classical music, while young people, who are usually more energetic and worked up, cannot stand it; they need the loud jarring beat of heavy metal.

Once I was looking through some of my video recordings where I was teaching self-control skills to different groups. And suddenly I noticed that the eyelids of a girl who was in a trance began to flutter ever so slightly, her eyeballs were moving up and down.

This phenomenon can be simulated artificially and in so doing arouse a trance.

The well-known method of American psychotherapist Francine Shapiro for treating psychological problems and emotional traumas with the help of eye movements is based on this connection between entry into a trance and fluctuations of the eyeballs.

Interesting information regarding the head movement technique

Sufi mystics have an element of head shaking in some of their rituals. There is also some disagreement about this; some believe that you should shake your head from side to side, while others believe it should be moved up and down. This just goes to show that one Key suits the first, while another the second.

Bulgarians, for example, shake their heads from left to right as a sign of agreement. When they shake their heads up and down, this means they disagree. It is probably easier for them to find the Key by shaking their head they way they do in agreement, because, when you are in agreement, you are more relaxed.

Haji-Murat's Finger

This technique has its story behind it. Once I was flying in an airplane and found myself sitting next to a friend of mine, Haji-Murat, an artist. He complained that we hardly ever see each other and asked me to teach him the Key techniques right there in the plane.

"Okay, let's begin," I replied, and asked him to concentrate on his index finger.

"You are an artist," I said, "and it will probably not be difficult for you to imagine your finger bending and straightening just as you wish. If you want to, close your eyes, however if your eyelids are tense, leave them open, but keep your eyes unfocused, as though you are looking at nothing."

He burst out laughing but began doing as I asked, and a minute later his finger did indeed begin slowly bending in small jerks.

My friend, amazed by this unusual phenomenon, began looking fascinated at the movement of his finger.

And…a minute later he was immersed in a trance.

Then he exclaimed, "You know what? I clearly saw one of my future paintings, now I want to paint it! How amazing!"

"That's all there is to it," I told Haji-Murat, "now you see that you can enter a state of free consciousness whenever you want and control your body. But before you needed special comfortable conditions, peace and quiet, complete concentration, many hours of training."

And I suggested that he repeat going in and out of this state to reinforce the skill.

A few minutes later he could already do it whenever he wished, and he began amusing himself with this game, carrying out various auto-suggestions in this state.

"I know how I can use this," he told me happily. "I can use to see my future paintings, I tried it just now, the themes are delightful! But why doesn't everyone do this, after all, it is so simple!"

"Salvador Dali did it. He tapped into his dreams by holding a pencil in his hand over a copper bowl and then allowing himself to fall asleep in front of his canvas."

"And why the pencil?"

"Just as he began to dream, his fingers would relax and let the pencil fall. The sound of it hitting the bowl woke him, and he would then draw or paint the fantastic images that had come to him during his dream state. You see how simple it is. He was a genius, he thought of it himself."

"Yes, very simple, and that is evidently why no one does it, because it is too simple for words."

The Aftereffect Stage

After doing the Star of Self-Control exercises for five days, you should sit each time and rest with an unfocused gaze. This is the Aftereffect Stage. Here you will reap the benefits of your efforts and enjoy that special feeling of inner lightness, peace, and harmony.

You should emerge from this comfortable state with a feeling of freshness. In order to do this you can complete the Aftereffect Stage by performing the basic Synchrogymnastic technique Slapping Your Back.

Continuing the Techniques

Next you will be able to use the selected Key or tension-releasing techniques both in combination with each other or separately.

For example, a short Synchrogymnastic workout of even one of the exercises you have selected yourself can be used before any demanding situation or emergency, it will immediately remove tension and give you a swift boost of self-confidence.

It is also recommended that the Synchrogymnastic be performed once every day in order to promote rapid health improvement and 2-3 times a day when you need to be in very good creative or physical form.

During the first five days, as indicated, you will gain experience in managing your state of wellbeing and develop an understanding of how to use the Key techniques for different goals.

Below you will find a guide for solving typical tasks. You can adapt and develop this guide to solve your own different problems.

Do not worry, you will be able to do it. You will quickly gain experience in using the method. It is like learning how to swim or ride a bike, once you learn the skill it will not be easy to forget. But you will be in charge of the way you do it, the direction you go in, and the motivation that prompts you.

Where Is the Payoff?

It often happens that daily life with its problems and pressures catches up with you again and you forget how you felt after you removed your stress. However, in order use the techniques to remove your stress the next time, you must be able to recall the positive experience you gained the first time.

Example

Consultation with an adolescent on Skype:

"You write that nothing changed after two weeks of doing the Synchrogymnastic exercises and levitation techniques. How are you feeling, do you feel better, has your tension decreased?"

"Tension? What do you mean?"

"You came to me with a problem, and I thought you must be feeling bad, do you feel better?"

"It seems I have always felt fine."

"Excuse me, but I found your letter, you wrote to me saying, 'I can't understand whether I am moving them apart myself or they are doing it on their own. There is no levitation of the arms and never was. I don't feel any delight or empty head, I only get more nervous because nothing particular is working, nothing new is happening, I still can't set any personal goals and I don't know what I really want. I was hoping for enlightenment, that I would remember how I used to be able to do things when I was a child that I can't do now! I really want to cry, I thought the Key was my last chance to change my life for the better, I am desperate, what should I do???'

"When I read your letter, I thought you must be in a bad way, since you talked about the chance of changing your life for the better. What mood are you in now?"

"Oh no, I am already much better. Now I am sure that everything is alright, and it will probably get better, I am in a more positive mood."

"I am glad that you are beginning to see some results, keep doing the exercises and you will reap even greater benefits. Bye for now.

Chapter 7.
The Synchromethod Is a New Era in Practical Psychology

The Key Method is very beneficial when patients cannot or do not want to share their concerns with a specialist, or, even though they could use some help, they do not want to discuss their problems with anyone.

Since the Key Method is not based on the choice of words, but on the choice of simple exercises that remove stress automatically, regardless of a person's attitude toward the techniques and the degree of his or her receptivity, it helps to quickly remove stress and open up contact between the patient and the specialist to then make verbal methods of correction and rehabilitation more effective.

The Key techniques even helped me to relieve children and adults suffering from severe stress after the terrorist acts in Beslan and other cities and achieve a dramatic and positive shift in their condition before my very eyes.

I have to say that in situations where there is very little time and a large number of victims, specialists—doctors and psychologists—are usually helpless; doctors, because there is not enough time to prescribe medication on an individual basis, and psychologists, because when under acute stress, victims are in an altered state of consciousness. This limits verbal contact between the specialist and patient and makes verbal psychological methods ineffective.

The positive role of the Key Method is particularly obvious in these conditions, since it affords ways to first establish psychological contact with the patients through physical movement before moving on to effective verbal methods of treatment, thus achieving rehabilitation of their psychophysiological state.

The author shows psychologists and rescue workers how to use the Key Method in their work

Key Techniques for Psychological Contact

Example 1

An adolescent who had been beaten up was unable to intelligibly describe what had happened, he stumbled over his words and could not put together a coherent sentence. He was under stress. The investigator-psychologist suggested he try the Key Stress Test to help calm him down.

The boy calmed down, related everything that had happened to him coherently and in detail, then sat down and suddenly fell asleep.

"He fell asleep," the investigator-psychologist, who was my student, told me. "Perhaps I made a mistake, is that not harmful?"

"It was a natural reaction. The boy was under stress, extremely worn out, so as soon as his stress was removed, he fell asleep. That's good. You were not only able to clarify the situation, but also help the boy to restore his equilibrium."

Example 2

A family categorically refused to communicate with doctors and social workers from the very beginning. The family was in mourning—two of their children had been killed in a terrorist act.

A group of specialists came to visit.

The mother of the deceased children, a woman of 35, was sitting immobile, her eyes downcast, to the left of her sat her mother, also immobile and silent. I went up to the mother of the children and without saying anything touched her shoulder, then I asked why she was holding her head in such an uncomfortable position, didn't her neck hurt? I gentle massaged her neck. I asked her to see if her neck was still hurting by moving her head. She did. Evidently, the pain in her neck had disappeared.

"And now raise both arms, hold them out in front of you, and imagine they are moving in opposite directions by themselves, automatically."

She did as she was asked. Her arms moved apart.

"And now stand up and try again." She stood up. Her arms moved apart.

"Now drop your arms and imagine they are rising up, levitating, imagine that your arms are wings like a bird in flight."

By reflex, she performed ideomotor movements similar to those in the Flight exercise. Her breathing became more even, freer, the muscles of her face relaxed and her cheeks took on a rosy glow. She responded to a smile with a smile.

"What do you do?"

"I am a nurse, I work in a maternity hospital."

"And I am a doctor, we will treat your mother together! We'll teach your mother how to fly."

The daughter showed her mother how to do the Key ideomotor techniques and described her own feelings, telling her how to mentally attune herself. After doing the Flight exercise, both women lost their constraint. They became more animated. On their own initiative, they called the dead children's father. Looking at them, he obediently sat down. He was extremely tense, constrained, silent, and performed the recommendations perfunctorily. He was able to do the exercise where his arms moved apart, but he refused to do the physical warm-up exercises. Two or three minutes after doing the first exercise, he began smiling. The family cheered up, the women began actively talking to the doctors, offering them tea.

"You are a nurse, you have many neighbors who lost close relatives, now you can help them, show them these anti-stress techniques; can you remember how to do them?"

"Yes, of course; and I will go and visit my neighbors, they really need this."

Example 3

A week ago a patient came to see me who had a tumor that required surgery. She came to learn the anti-stress training techniques, understanding that this would help the surgery to go smoother and the post-surgery period to be more effective.

I showed her the discharge techniques.

Unfortunately, she was unable for other reasons to come to see me again and called me on the phone.

She said that she had been doing the discharge exercises for three days morning and evening and afterwards felt calm and relaxed, but 2-3 hours later she would again begin having disturbing thoughts.

She was unable to come and see me for consultation again, and the surgery was in three days.

I told her that it was a pity she was unable to do the procedure in my office a second time, but I gave her advice over the phone.

"Now," I told her, "after Discharge, you need to do Recharge. If you were in a minus state at the beginning and could not think any positive thoughts, now you have removed some of your tension and can think positively. If you allowed your thoughts to take their own course during Discharge and reached zero, now, when you begin the exercise, think positive thoughts, think about how the surgery will be successful and after the surgery you will recover very quickly. And, most important," I told her, "attune yourself not only for the day of the surgery, but look further ahead. Your surgery is on Thursday, but think about Friday and Saturday, about how quickly you are going to recover. The further ahead you look and plan, the better. And today, after this Recharge, you will already be in a good mood and sleep better, and tomorrow you will feel even better still."

"But how can I think in the zero state?" she asked.

"Think until you reach zero, because during the zero state you will not want to think about anything. You will disappear into that emptiness in your head and new connections will be created in the brain. They will support you. After you have done the procedure, call me."

And indeed, after the procedure she phoned me in a good mood and said that she was feeling much more confident.

Example 4

The mother of an adolescent phoned me and said that her son was shaking in fear and she did not know what to do with him. I suggested she call an ambulance because doctors should not give advice without seeing the patient.

She said that she had called an ambulance, but while she was waiting for it to arrive, she must urgently do something to help her son. I asked her to let me talk to him.

He said that he had been in a cafü with some friends and that he thought someone had put something into his glass of wine. Now he was worried that this had in fact happened.

"But why do you think someone did that?" I asked.

"They are always joking about it," he said, "and now, after I got home, I suddenly became convinced that perhaps they weren't joking and became very afraid and my blood pressure shot up to 180."

I suggested that he sway back and forth standing where he was with the telephone in his hand.

He did that and said he wanted to go to sleep. I suggested he lie down, and soon his mother phoned and said he was asleep, his blood pressure had returned to normal. The ambulance came, the medics checked him out and, after satisfying themselves that his condition was stable, they left. So everything turned out well.

It is important to remember that this kind of therapy is not a substitute for professional medical advice or treatment for specific medical conditions and you should always seek the advice of your physician or other qualified health care provider with any questions you may have regarding a medical condition; however there are times when a psychologist can also give advice long distance and achieve the necessary result.

I would like to draw your attention to the fact that in these examples, I was engaging in psychotherapy with these patients using the Discharge and Recharge techniques.

A physician can also practice this kind of psychotherapy using other Key techniques depending on the circumstances, and psychotherapy in combination with the Key techniques is extremely effective, which patients can later repeat on their own.

Crisis center workers can also use the Key techniques to provide more efficient assistance during telephone consultations with patients who call the hotline since these exercises are very simple to perform and quickly yield a positive result.

So the Key is heralding in a new era in practical psychology.

Chapter 8.
Synchrogymnastics
Increase Your Health, Creativity, and
Longevity in Five Minutes

Synchrogymnastics differ from ordinary physical exercises in that they are performed on the basis of movements that synchronize with your current state of wellbeing, so they generate an instant freeing effect accompanied by a strong boost in self-confidence.

They are a high-powered way to improve your health and rapidly achieve and maintain an optimal state of equilibrium in changing conditions while simultaneously activating the additional mental and physical reserves necessary for making effectual decisions.

If you do not have the time or desire to devote to long and strenuous physical exercises, try Synchrogymnastics. In just five minutes, they will afford you with the same therapeutic effect you would normally achieve after an hour of aerobics.

The first Synchrogymnastics technique, Slapping Your Back, alone yields immediate results: your head clears, you want to walk up straight with your shoulders thrown back, you feel a surge of self-confidence, and you are ready to do things that previously seemed beyond you.

This new super workout has already been included in a physical education textbook published in Russia for school children.

All five Synchrogymnastics exercises bring about positive mental changes that help you to tackle any problem you may be facing.

It is also recommended that you add your own movements to these basic exercises as you feel the need. This will bring your mental and physical processes into harmony, thus raising the quality of your intellectual capabilities.

For example, when performing the second exercise, the Cross-Country Skier, you may also feel the need to rise up and down on the balls of your feet as you move your arms up and down. Go ahead!

Like any warm-up, tension-releasing exercise, Synchrogymnastics stimulate the production of endorphins—the biological foundation of positive emotions that participate in restoration and self-healing of the body—and improve the blood flow to the brain and internal organs.

> **Tip for achieving synchronization between the repetitive movements and your current inner state: Think about a problem that is bothering you and, in so doing, perform the movements you find easiest. This helps you to find the rhythm and movement that are best suited to you individually and to solving your personal problems.**

Technique Tips:

1. Choose a rhythm and movement that quickly becomes automatic;

2. When you do, your tension will dissipate and you will want to keep on doing this repetitive movement;

3. Let your thoughts come as they will and soon the chaos in your head will subside and your thoughts will become directed toward achieving your desired goal.

Personal Example

Recently at the World Yachting Championships in Cascais (Portugal), to which President of the Yachting Federation and Russian Presidential Representative in the Russian Federation Council Alexander Kotenkov invited me, the following incident occurred.

I arrived at the championships at a low point—the team had already taken part in the races, so arranging a training session seemed pointless, and they had lost, so no one was interested in learning new methods, particularly from someone they did not know. The Russian team has strong athletes, among them are many-time world and European champions, but they had lost. I felt even more uncomfortable because Kotenkov had introduced me as the team's "secret weapon." I was in a quandary.

Ready to give up in the midst of the general disappointment over the lost races, I was in need of the Key Method myself.

I stood in my hotel room and performed the Cross-Country Skier exercise from Synchrogymnastics, thinking perplexedly, "What should I do? What should I do?"

Suddenly, toward the end of the first minute, all chaotic thoughts disappeared, and in the free field of consciousness that opened up within me, the answer clearly appeared in bold relief: "You don't know what to do? How's that? What did you come here for? To help these guys? So go and help them!"

And I felt strong and confident.

I knocked at the door of the room where the tired team members were resting after their ordeal out on the water and spontaneously found the right words to bring them to their feet. The athletes stood up and began energetically doing the S Synchrogymnastic.

The next day, another group of athletes began learning the Key.

A few days later, one of them said that he noticed that whenever he was able to do the Key Stress Test easily in the morning, he had a good day.

And after that even Anna Stepanova, who was suffering from a knee injury, went out to sea and courageously took part in a yachting race. Yachtsmen will understand the immense effort this took in her condition.

The basic course for learning Synchrogymnastics requires between three and five 30-minute individual or group training sessions.

As a result, you will be able to choose your own individual style for performing these exercises.

It is recommended that you perform the Synchrogymnastics regularly for 5 minutes every day, whenever is convenient for you. The exercises can also be performed separately, depending on your goal and the result you want to achieve.

It is easy to explain Synchrogymnastics and show a live audience how to do them, but very difficult to describe them in a book. Nor do photographs of the exercises express the nuances of the internal work that evokes the clear beneficial effect of these unique exercises.

Like any new activity, Synchrogymnastics should, if possible, be learned under the supervision of a specialist who has undergone special training.

Synchrogymnastics Consist of Five Simple Exercises

Slapping Your Back
The Cross-Country Skier
Twisting
Bending
Easy Dance

Each of these exercises has a psychological effect in addition to its physical benefit.

1. Slapping Your Back, for example, is for loosening up and mobilization and for increasing your energy and self-confidence before any demanding situation—an important meeting, negotiations, exam, or competition, for example.

2. The Cross-Country Skier is for making level-headed decisions.

3. Twisting helps you to calm down, relax, and discharge.

4. Bending is used to raise your self-confidence, loosen muscles, and develop flexibility of the spine.

5. Easy Dance helps to develop coordination, raise mental stability, and develop flexibility in the lumbar section of the spine.

All the Synchrogymnastics exercises are coordinated with each other so that the previous exercise is the foundation for more successful performance of the next exercise. This inter-coordination makes it possible for almost anyone to very quickly be able to bend and touch the floor or easily perform the difficult-to-coordinate movements in the Easy Dance exercise.

Slapping Your Back

Slapping Your Back is an exercise that creates an instantaneous freeing effect in 30-40 seconds. It is based on our instinctive behavior in stressful situations. What do people do in the cold, for example, to release tension and warm up? They slap their arms while synchronously stamping their feet. The repetitive movement performed naturally corresponds to the level of tension—the higher the tension, the more frequent and energetic the slapping.

But can we expect anyone to think about using this slapping technique before sitting an exam, taking part in a competition, or engaging in important talks? It is unlikely, because these movements are associated with the cold, while exams demand intellectual effort, although limbering up is just as beneficial for both chess players and weight lifters.

Slap your back for 30 seconds to one minute.

Keep your arms loose and floppy like a rag doll.

You should not try to force them, but just throw them freely across your chest.

Throw your arms across your chest and around your back easily, freely, slappingly! Try to throw them as far around your back as you can, so that your palms freely slap your shoulder blades, giving the characteristic sound of a slap.

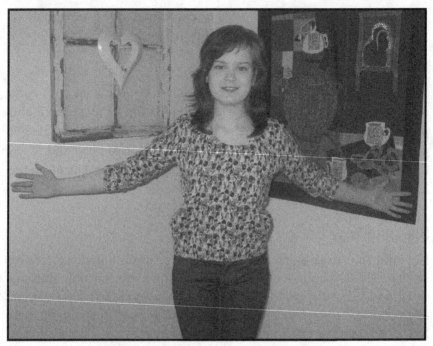

Slapping your back

Throw your arms across your chest and around your back

Begin slowly, do not beat yourself too hard, it should all be done gradually. In a month or two, you will be able to slap hard and with pleasure.

This loosens up your neck and chest muscles, which improves blood flow to the brain, particularly venous return. When you begin the slapping movement, the tops of your lungs come together, contract, and when you swing your arms apart, your lungs draw apart and expand too. This stimulation of the lungs creates the effect of a pump that arouses intensive enrichment of the blood with oxygen.

In just 30-40 seconds, your head will clear and you will feel invigorated.

There are reflex zones in the shoulder-blade area where you are slapping yourself which are known in medicine as Zakharin-Head zones, the stimulation of which arouses an intensive flow of nerve impulses to the brain and spinal chord. Slapping Your Back also generates the same effect as slapping yourself with birch leaves after a sauna, as is the Russian custom, and many other beneficial effects.

The main prerequisite, I repeat, is to slap yourself on the back without any effort, keeping your arms loose and throwing them around as though you were a rag doll.

Or you can choose another image that suits you better, image your arms are tree branches swaying in the wind, for example.

If you do the Slapping technique before facing a demanding situation, think about what awaits you as you perform the slapping movements. This is how a boxer prepares himself for a fight, by turning over in his mind the movements he will make, and the body chooses the frequency of repetitive slapping movements itself.

If you use the Slapping exercise in ordinary situations, do not rush, imagine that you are standing under a pleasantly warm or refreshing shower or waterfall.

When you do take a shower, make a mental note of the pleasant sensations it arouses in order to recall them later while doing this exercise.

Doing the Slapping exercise every day as part of the five-minute Synchrogymnastics will improve your ability to loosen up and release your tension.

You can use these skills in situations you face every day by doing the Slapping exercise in your head whenever you need to remove tension and increase your self-confidence. Just visualize yourself doing the exercise, and in 10-20 seconds you will find yourself in a positive frame of mind.

The Cross-Country Skier

Begin by standing comfortably with your body relaxed, your feet slightly apart, and your arms hanging loosely by your sides.

The exercise is called the Cross-Country Skier because the repetitive movements in it, although not directly, are reminiscent of the movements of a cross-country skier. However, you should not take this literally, since the main idea of the Key Method is to choose your own movements and rhythms, ones that best correspond to the way you are currently feeling.

In this exercise, you will swing your arms up and down while synchronously rising onto the balls of your feet and back down again, or vice versa.

The type of movement is completely arbitrary and of your own choice; you can swing your arms up and down while keeping your back straight, or if it is more comfortable, you can bend your back slightly, or even bend right down to the floor, like a skier going downhill.

Swing your arms up and then bring them down. As your arms come back down, you rise onto the balls of your feet in synchrony with the downward motion of your arms, then bring your heels back down until they strike the floor.

These rhythmic strikes of the heels against the floor are essentially a combination of the Cross-Country Skier exercise and the well-known method created by Academician Alexander Mikulin, who describes this technique for improving the vascular system, which he calls vibrogymnastics, in his book *Aktivnoe dolgoletie* (Active Longevity).

A well-known Russian aircraft engine designer, Mikulin gave great significance to the valves of the body's vascular system, practiced vibrogymnastics himself for several decades, and was in superb mental and physical health. This is how Alexander Mikulin describes vibrogymnastics: "...Lift your heels off the ground to about 1 cm, you don't need to go higher. Drop your heels back to the floor without too much force. You might want to keep your teeth pressed together to minimize negative feelings from vibrations in your head. The same thing happens when you run or walk. The veins in your legs have valves which only let your blood flow in one direction – upward: from the toes to the thighs. When your heels hit the ground the blood passes through the valves and makes it to the heart. Repeat this exercise about 30 times, and make sure you wait at least one second between repetitions. If you do it too fast the blood will not have time to accumulate between the valves.

"After you are done with your first set, take a 10-second break and repeat. Perform this exercise 4-5 times a day."

A. Mikulin goes on to write:

"…in addition to being beneficial for those who sit or stand for long periods of time, vibrogymnastics should also be used whenever you have to perform prolonged mental activities. The pressure these exercises creates counteracts the stall of blood flow and energetically moves venal blood from the head to the heart, thus relieving the heaviness often felt in the head during intense intellectual work.

"Vibrogymnastics can also be used to counteract fatigue when climbing a hill, for example. I recommend doing this exercise for one minute every 150-200 m of your uphill climb. It is particularly effective for removing fatigue during long walks."

Academic Mikulin also writes that if you live in a climatic zone that has snow, choose skiing as your sport. Cross-country skiing has a positive effect on all the muscle groups of the body at the same time and is also conducive to weight loss. And who does not feel more confident with a taut and slender body, not to mention all the other health benefits…

So when doing the Cross-Country Skier exercise, you get the benefit of a unique combination of both this exercise and Alexander Mikulin's vibrogymnastics. Choose the way you move your arms and legs yourself according to the Key principles, do what feels most comfortable, what comes easiest and with the least effort in order to obtain the greatest effect. Maybe you will find it easier to do it the other way around, rising up on the balls of your feet while raising your arms, and bringing them back down as you lower your arms. This is not important. The main thing is to coordinate the movements and how energetically you do them, doing them more vigorously the higher the level of your tension. But do not overdo it, particularly if you have bone spurs or back problems. All medication is only beneficial in the right dose. And the Cross-Country Skier exercise, which includes vibrogymnastics, also has a therapeutic effect; the vibrational irritants are perceived by the surface, skin, and deep-seated sensatory receptors. They transfer information about this irritant to the peripheral and central nervous system, which stimulates vascular vitality, preventing venal stagnation. And increased blood circulation activates the body's metabolism.

Doing the Cross-Country Skier exercise for one minute every day along with the other Synchrogymnastics techniques helps to improve your overall health. But, in addition, just like Slapping Your Back, it can be done separately when necessary, while thinking over a difficult problem in order to make a level-headed decision, for example. After just one minute of virtual skiing in a rhythm you enjoy, you will begin to feel your chaotic thoughts settling to reveal a calm and confident view of the future and all your initial problems will seem to take care of themselves. When your head is clear and you feel invigorated, it is always easier to find the optimal solution.

Twisting

This third exercise in Synchrogymnastics is the easiest to describe.

You may remember doing this as a child, twisting from left to right, just using your body while keeping your feet firmly planted on the ground and allowing your arms to flop freely as though you were a rag doll. The higher the nervous tension, the more energetic the twisting.

Stand with your feet comfortably apart, your arms hanging loosely by your sides and twist from left to right in an easy and relaxed way for one minute in a rhythm you do not want to stop.

Stand, twist, and think about your problems.

You will notice that while you are doing this exercise and thinking about something that is worrying you or about your other trials and tribulations, or about some upcoming meeting, about anything at all, you will gradually begin thinking about all these things in a much calmer way. Emotional distancing is occurring.

Doing this exercise for one minute as part of your daily five-minute workout will noticeably bolster your nervous system and develop your body's mobility, loosen your back muscles, and add flexibility to your spine.

This exercise can also be done separately.

Do this for 5-10 minutes at any time that is convenient for you and you will notice that you become calmer, more balanced, wiser, and it is easier for you to deal with your fears. Moreover, the exercise helps to get rid of dizziness.

Twisting from right to left   *Twisting from left to right*

For example, the weather has changed, things are going wrong, or you are just in for a difficult day, stand up and twist for 5-10 minutes. As you do the exercise, it will become easier and more enjoyable to do with each passing minute because your tension is decreasing.

By doing the exercise for different lengths of time, you can obtain different effects.

For example, if you are unable to fall asleep, you can do this exercise before you go to bed as a kind of Lullaby. In this case, you need to do the exercise for a longer length of time, for 15-20 minutes, for example.

And this is what we do in bed when we cannot sleep, we toss and turn from one side to the other.

But you can do this before you go to bed, helping your mind to scan more quickly over the emotional points of the day and, after you have removed your tension, you will fall asleep much more easily and quickly.

And you will awaken in the morning with a clear head!

Just like when you were a child and ran around all day in the fresh air, you will get into bed, snuggle down in the warm blankets, and sleep like a baby! And you will awaken rested and full of strength and energy! It is the morning of a new day; a new day that awaits you with all kinds of pleasant surprises and revelations.

It will not be like today, when you did not get enough sleep, when you woke up and the morning did not herald the inspiration of a new day, but felt like the continuation of yesterday, one long gray and monotonous tunnel.

In order to retain a feeling of eternal youth and health and keep your brain agile and active, you need to keep the child in you alive.

This technique can be performed for an even longer time if you need to release accumulated tension and free yourself from unpleasant thoughts and impressions. This is no longer a Lullaby, but Discharge-Recharge, or the Mill, which pulverizes mental traumas and problems by means of repetitive movements, like millstones grinding grain into flour.

The length of time it takes to do this exercise is determined by how long it takes to reach zero, through which automatic recharge of the brain occurs to reach a positive frame of mind. And zero, as you already know from this book, occurs when movements become automatic and your head empty, that is, emotional distancing.

Then it is as though you have been reborn!

Bending

This exercise is part of anti-stress training, it builds mental stability by learning how to keep the neck muscles loose in tense situations.

Bending is an exercise for both the mind and the body.

First, let's take a look at what happens in a situation when you encounter a problem.

Tension arises to activate the resources needed to resolve the problem.

First the neck muscles, which are particularly prone to the impact of stress, tense up and could go into spasms. If you were asked to sit down, sensors were attached to your body, and you were given a newspaper to read, as soon as your attention is attracted by some disturbing piece of news, the neck sensors would be the first to react.

This is why most people feel pain in their neck. Constant tension gives rise to osteochondrosis and vegetative-vascular dystonia. And this, in turn, keeps the vessels tensed up.

Blocks create a viscous circle, whereby even a banal problem can arouse stress, causing narrowed consciousness, fear, complexes, and impoverished creativity due to stereotypical thinking. You can see how closely intertwined the mental and physiological processes are; not getting enough sleep may cause you to choose a stereotypical solution to an important task, while your ability to keep your neck muscles relaxed increases your self-confidence and allows the brain to act faster to come up with ingenious solutions. It is important to learn how to stop the neck muscles from seizing up at the critical moment, so that at tense moments your inner resources are activated in time and used to successfully resolve your problems.

The fourth Synchrogymnastics exercise is designed to simulate tension by holding an uncomfortable position and training the neck muscles to remain loose at times of tension.

This position in and of itself is a beneficial all-round strengthening and health-improving exercise for developing flexibility of the spine and efficient functioning of the internal organs. This exercise will help you to ward off illness and retain your self-confidence regardless of the circumstances you encounter.

Stand with your feet shoulder-width apart and bend backward to form a half-bridge.

Practicing Bending

This is only the first part of the exercise, bending back, while there are four parts altogether—bending back, bending forward, releasing tension, and touching the floor.

At first do not try to bend back too far. You will be able to do that in a couple of months.

As you bend back, your abdomen tenses up and becomes hard on its own in the same way as it would if you were doing sit-ups. But now you can do this in a more natural way, just bend backwards and hold it.

You can slap yourself on your stomach and feel happy!

Your abdomen is tense and hard! You feel satisfied. This position stimulates proper functioning of the intestines and all the internal organs; it helps women to establish hormonal balance and restore the menstrual cycle; it frees you from pain and constipation and helps to burn off extra fatty tissue.

But first do this exercise, like all the others, gradually, without forcing yourself. Remember the golden rule: easy does it!

It is not comfortable to stand this way. While holding this uncomfortable position, remember the discomfort and tension you felt the first time so you can compare it with how you will feel in literally thirty seconds after your neck loosens up.

Think about how you stretch in the morning when you wake up or how you did this as a child after a good sleep. You instinctively performed part of the exercise you are doing now. Begin to loosen up your neck by moving it in ways that are natural for you, stretching it from left to right, do what feels most comfortable for you, as though you are removing your head from its neck rest. This does not require a lot of effort.

Suddenly you will feel that something has changed as your neck loosens up.

Is it easier to hold the position? Indeed it is!

To finish this part of the exercise, stretch as you would normally do in the morning upon rising.

This is the first part of the exercise—bending back.

The second part is bending forward.

Bend over and allow your arms to hang loosely, letting the tension drain out of them, relax, and let yourself go.

Now begin the third part by directing your attention to the small of your back and relaxing the muscles.

Do this is synchrony with your breathing, whatever you find most comfortable, as you breathe in or breathe out, relax the muscles of your back. You are removing a barrier. This is how you gain control over tension in uncomfortable conditions. And only then, when you feel the muscles give way and relax, when the block has been removed, continue freely bending forward, trying to touch the floor.

This is the fourth part of the exercise—touching the floor.

Do not try to reach the floor the very first time, do it gradually. You may be able to this in just a few days, although many healthy people, particularly women, can do it immediately regardless of their body build.

You will be amazed at your achievements!

However, you should remember that Slapping Your Back, the Cross-Country Skier, and Twisting all helped to achieve this.

Then return to your initial position, standing as normal.

This exercise takes about one minute in the total set of Synchrogymnastics.

Do not rush, in one minute you can do this exercise two or three times, the main thing is to attune yourself to removing the block in the small of your back when bending forward.

And notice that even while repeating the exercise during one session, it becomes easier to bend backward and forward.

I would like to explain some more why adding additional movements, loosening up movements of the head, does not arouse additional difficulties in such an uncomfortable pose, on the contrary, you feel amazing release.

Jacques Mayol, the first free diver to descend to 100 meters, expounds his theories on reaching a state of mind based on relaxation in his book *Homo Delphinus—The Dolphin Within Man*. The main thing was to switch his attention. When he held his breath and concentrated his attention on holding his breath, it was very difficult to do. But if he held his breath while concentrating on the base of his spine, the root chakra, which is where the Kundalini, the Primal Life Force for all of Creation, is stored, holding his breath became automatic and he could do it with much less effort.

The way I see it, the crux of the matter is precisely in switching the attention, emotional distancing, during which the body solves the task it has been set.

On the other hand, the Kundalini moving from the root chakra along the spinal column to the crown was a powerful image which helped Jacques Mayol to switch his attention. Jacques Mayol regards this chakra as a source of the body's reserve energy.

Using this example, we again see how effective emotional distancing is in resolving problems, an approach where the Ego with its fears, complexes, and stereotypes does not interfere with the body, formed over millions of years of evolution, responding reflexively to the changes we visualize and wish to achieve.

This is harmony of mind and body, which in the ancient Indian language of Sanskrit is called Yoga.

So as you do the Bending exercise think about how much it will help you to resolve all your vitally important problems.

Easy Dance

The fifth Synchrogymnastics exercise is based on the relation between coordination and mental stability. Cats, for example, always fall on their paws, they are difficult to command, they do as they please. If you want to train your coordination, first, this exercise will immediately show the degree to which you are ready to perform coordinated or uncoordinated movements and, second, it will raise your inner harmony and, correspondingly, your harmony with the outside world, as well as develop your mental stability.

But in order to be able to easily perform some difficult movement, you need an image to guide you, like an orchestra conductor.

The image that comes to my mind is Easy Dance—complicated movements on the count of four: one-two-three-four, and that's it! I am back to the beginning, to my initial position.

Stand with your feet together, your arms hanging by your side.

One – step forward with your right foot.

Two – swing your left leg to the right, putting your weight on your right foot and rising up on the ball of this foot while turning your body to the right and swinging your arms slightly to the right.

Your back twists, make sure you do not do this too abruptly, be gentle on your back.

Three – bring your left leg, arms and body back to their original position.

Dr. Aliev teaching the Easy Dance to nurses

Four – step back with your right foot to the original position, that is, to the position from where you began the first movement.

Repeat 3-4 times.

Then perform the same movement on your other foot.

One – step forward with your left foot.

Two – swing you right leg to the left, putting your weight on your left foot and rising up on the ball of this foot while turning to the left and slightly swinging your arms to the left.

Three – bring your leg, arms and body back to the original position.

Four – step back with the left foot to the original position.

Repeat 3-4 times.

When you figure out the left from the right, it will take you one minute to do this exercise.

Now you have a whole set of tools for self-control and you can use them depending on the task facing you.

First, you have the Key Stress Test to check your level of tension at any time.

Second, if you are tense, you can do the Slapping Your Back exercise to remove excess tension and inhibition.

You can also use this Stress Test in another way—the ideomotor techniques activate self-control, creating a frame of mind in which you can work on yourself by thinking about the changes you want to make in yourself and in your life—the Key to unlocking new capabilities in yourself.

And third, you have the Synchrogymnastics, which you can do for 5 minutes a day any time you want or before undertaking any intense and demanding task to maintain your inner equilibrium.

The entire system is designed to help you cope with the stress caused by the different problems you encounter in your life, raise your confidence in yourself, get your bearings faster, retain your energy, choose better solutions, and learn to find that inner equilibrium any time you need to deal with a particular issue.

And you will immediately notice that the world has become a simpler, more understandable, and friendlier place. And most important, you have a sense of inner freedom, confident in the knowledge that you know just what, when, and how to do what you need to do.

Now that you have found the Key to yourself, you can unlock the abandon and freedom you felt as a child, before you became burdened by the responsibilities and phobias of adulthood. The inner equilibrium you have acquired with the help of the Key provides you with a source of wisdom. And now, with the skills to manage your own inner state and wellbeing, you are free again. By combining your adult experience and intellect with the inhibition you felt as a child, you can now think and act not only with free abandon, but also with wise conscientiousness.

Rehabilitation of the fire victims in the Nizhny Novgorod Region. The exercises begin

The exercises end. How wonderful!

Chapter 9.
Two Trusty Helpers

Scanning

If you are internally tense, or you feel anxious, or you are unable to do the Key techniques, you can use one of these additional exercises. They are chosen by trying each of the Scanning exercises in turn.

You will spend one minute on each exercise.

You need to choose the exercise that most quickly creates a natural and comfortable state of mental and physical equilibrium.

This exercise can be used either separately or together with other exercises, thus making the entire set more effective. It might be beneficial to do it between Key exercises or in combination with Yoga or Qigong exercises, meditation, or as part of any other training or health-improvement programs and capability development techniques you practice.

Scanning exercises are chosen based on the Key principle, that is, by synchronizing the movement and your current state of being.

> **Tips for making your individual choice of exercise: choose the movement that is the most comfortable to perform and that quickly becomes automatic as you repeat it.**

This set of exercises is called Scanning because, as you perform them, you scan your body from top to bottom with the help of repetitive rhythmic movements and find the movement that removes stress in a matter of seconds.

I repeat, when choosing the exercise that is right for you, pick the one that you can do with the least effort, in a rhythm that you want to keep on doing.

1. For one minute, do any easy and pleasant movements that involve turning the head, choosing movements that are comfortable.

2. For one minute, do any easy and pleasant repetitive movements at the shoulder level. You can swing your arms, perform rotary movements of your shoulders, pretend you are swimming, rowing, and so on, whatever you find easiest and most enjoyable.

3. For one minute, do any easy and pleasant repetitive rotating movements at the hip level, as though you were spinning a hoop, belly dancing, and so on, speeding up and slowing down the rhythm to find the one most comfortable for you.

4. For one minute, do any easy and pleasant repetitive movements at the knee level, either rotating them, doing slight knee bends, or bending and straightening by rising up and down on the balls of your feet.

5. And now stop, rest, and think about which of the repetitive movements was most comfortable to do.

Repeat this exercise for several minutes.

Remember the feeling of comfort so that you can recall it in the future.

Emerge from this pleasant state feeling invigorated.

The movement you did just now is your individual warm-up exercise.

Perhaps this movement is something you do automatically, without thinking about it, whenever you feel tense, so it will immediately feel familiar to you.

Now, with your new awareness, you will be able to remove tension and feel comfortable whenever you need to just by visualizing the movements, without actually doing the exercise.

Tip. If you want, you can dose out the tension-releasing effect by regulating the time you do the exercise you have chosen; the longer you do the exercise, the more relaxed you will become, from being stressed to loosening up and on to calming down and deep relaxation.

Ideomotor Vibrogymnastics

This exercise takes from 30-40 seconds. It removes nervous jitters, fear, and fatigue.

Athletes can use it before the start of a race to remove prestart jitters and raise their self-confidence.

You can free yourself from nervous jitters by performing rhythmic vibrational movements of the body that resonate with your internal nervous jitters, as though giving free rein to the jitters and allowing them to flow through your body.

When you find a resonating rhythm and automatic movements, tension and fatigue disappear almost instantly because your internal organs and body systems are working in harmony.

This exercise is beneficial for people who lead a sedentary way of life accompanied by high levels of emotional tension.

It helps to get rid of fatigue, feel invigorated, remove the feeling of heaviness in the head that appears after intense intellectual effort, and eliminate vascular and muscular spasms.

Ideomotor vibrogymnastics can be practiced as a separate independent exercise or as an auxiliary means for achieving better performance of the Key techniques.

Vibrogymnastics are most effective when you are under extreme stress or severely fatigued.

The most important thing is choosing a rhythm of vibrational movements that is right for you. I repeat, a rhythm should be chosen that quickly becomes automatic. When this happens, you are able to perform the vibrational movements with minimum effort in a rhythm that is so enjoyable you do not want to stop.

> **Try to find an exercise that is comfortable to do. People with back problems should not do these ideomotor vibrogymnastics without consulting a doctor.**

If you do the exercise gently, without too much vigor, it will quickly help you to loosen up and remove fatigue when working at the computer, for example. After doing this exercise for 30-40 seconds, you can continue working efficiently for a few more hours.

Stand straight, relax, raise your shoulders and move them gently up and down as though you were riding a horse.

Begin the vibrational movements from your knees using your entire body, bending and straightening both knees at the same time, as though doing slight knee bends.

At first, speed up the bending and flexing of your knees in search of the rhythm you find most comfortable, then you can slow the movements down again. While doing this, keep the upper part of the body relaxed, your arms and shoulders should move freely in rhythm with your entire body.

Use visualization to help you find your rhythm more easily; imagine you are riding a horse, or that a powerful vibromassager is attached to your relaxed body.

After one or two attempts you will find the rhythm that suits you best, the one that will immediately put you in the saddle, so to speak, without having to keep looking for the right frequency of vibrational movements.

Vibrogymnastics raises your body's capacity for responding to your own willful commands, so try repeating to yourself 5-7 times, "I am healthy, calm, I have tons of energy, I am full of strength, everything will be alright!" And you will see that it works!

Chapter 10.
When and How to Use the Key Method

1.   When you know what you want;

2.   When you want to figure out what you want.

In the first case, when you know what you want, you simply visualize what you wish to achieve as you are going the Key techniques and your body will begin to activate the inner resources necessary to make it a reality.

In the second case, when you want to figure out and understand what you want, you perform Key techniques that induce a state of mental and physical equilibrium and as your mind and body are brought into harmony, you begin to clearly see what it is you really want.

Example

Maxim knew what he wanted. He was preparing for a competition and in order to win he needed to work on a new movement in his jump, which, when nervous, he always did wrong. Using the Key techniques, he induced a state of mental and physical equilibrium, went into a light trance by repeating the techniques, and then visualized performing the jump perfectly.

While in this frame of mind, Maxim could easily visualize himself performing a perfect jump.

At the next training session in the gym, he performed the jump in practice as he had visualized it, then once at home again, reinforced his newly learned skills by visualizing his perfectly performed moves.

In this way, by practicing the jump using two essentially different methods, in practice in the gym and in his mind using the Key techniques, he shortened the road to success.

An Amusing, but Useful Example

Two girlfriends came to see me; they wanted to use the Key techniques to learn a foreign language after reading in my book that this method helps you to become uninhibited, removes the fear of making a mistake, and speeds up the development of the desirable verbal skills by eliminating old stereotypes.

However, one of the girls did not come to the second session.

I phoned her and asked what had happened, did she not find the techniques useful?

"No, that's not it at all! I am very grateful to you. I have been using your method, I did the twisting exercise at home, calmed down, and then I realized ...

"The thing is that it's my friend who is going to Canada with her husband in two months, she urgently needs to learn English, but I'm not going anywhere, I don't really need any language skills. It's just I let my friend's enthusiasm carry me away and thought I had to urgently learn English too. I went around like a mad thing for two weeks, gathering all kinds of books to help me learn, but now, thanks to your method, I've seen the light. I realized this is not what I need to be doing at the moment. Thank you for helping me to see this, I'll learn English some other time."

Do You Know What You Want?

The Key Method has two vectors of development—vertical and horizontal.

The vertical is strategic, it involves working on who you want to be. This is the vector of your conscious evolution, your Life Line.

The horizontal vector, on the other hand, helps you to find the solution using the Key Method to millions of the most diverse and applied problems, from removing stress, headaches, and fatigue to quickly learning a foreign language.

So first let me talk about the vertical vector of strategy.

For at least five minutes, leave whatever you are doing and visualize in your mind's eye the person you want to be.

After this, you will continue visualizing the ideal you wish to achieve as you perform the Key exercises, and, in so doing, the image in your mind will become a tuning fork that activates the necessary changes in your body.

To form your ideal image, you will need to be creative, visualizing yourself as you want to be.

Draw a picture of yourself in your mind's eye, like an artist, lavishly throwing on the color.

This is already psychotherapy in itself, but in combination with the Key techniques it becomes extremely effective.

What feeling of inner lightness would you like to achieve?

What kind of figure would you like have? Deportment? Way of walking? Mannerisms?

Visualize yourself moving gracefully, smiling charmingly, laughing genuinely, dancing wonderfully, singing magnificently, performing brilliantly before an audience.

What about the way you look and the pitch of your voice, your character traits, qualities and capabilities?

Try closing your eyes for a moment and visualizing yourself in full splendor, in a wonderful mood and full of energy.

You may find that internal fears, stereotypical thinking, complexes, and other psychological barriers interfere with this creative visualization.

If so, try activating the Discharge process with the help of which you can quickly remove tension and reach zero. Choose any repetitive movement, just letting your thoughts come as they will. When your head feels empty and you find you could not care less about anything that used to bother you, sit down and rest for a while. Then, with a clear head, do Recharge, attuning yourself to positive emotions.

For example, try as she might, one patient who suffered from various ailments just could not imagine herself healthy, while another, who was used to stooping, could not imagine himself with a straight back. They made long and unproductive rounds of the doctors, undergoing massage, doing acupuncture, and taking medication without any tangible results. But how can treatment help if a person has convinced himself that he is sick and ailing?

Processes at the subconscious level may also interfere with creative thinking. For example, you want to be slim and elegant, but your mind dishes up your customary image of yourself, telling you that you are plump and frumpy.

The Key techniques will help you to remove psychological barriers in order to overcome these and other stereotypes that prevent you from moving forward.

Your body is capable of tuning into any program activated in the brain like a radio receiver tunes into the wave of a radio station. As you visualize yourself as strong and healthy, you are activating a positive attitude that synthesizes and unifies within you the effect of everything you undertake to improve your health, be it physical exercises, massage, acupuncture, or medication.

As you read these recommendations, you are already working on visualizing your ideal, and when you repeat this visualization as you practice the Key techniques, you will be rewarded with tangible results, what you visualize becomes a reality.

Personal Example

Until I started using the Key, I would never have believed that I could become an artist.

It would never have entered my head, because I always got Cs in school for drawing, while my friend got As, and his parents were artists.

I often heard people talk about the throes of creativity, that you cannot achieve anything without effort, that nothing worth having comes easy, that art requires sacrifice, that Van Gogh was the tortured genius who even cut off his ear in his suffering, and so on. And I was inflicted by a mental block: I am not an artist and will never be one. This avenue of creativity is closed to me forever.

I would use the Key to remove the anxiety and fears that sometimes arose due to vascular spasms from working too hard or from chronic lack of sleep.

Then I saw the paintings of my friend Rakhman, I liked them, and I also wanted to paint. I decided to use the Key to remove the barrier I had created in my mind about my inability to paint and, while doing the Key techniques, imagined myself painting only masterpieces.

And I did not come up against any inner resistance; my inner voice said, if you want to paint, go ahead and paint!

So I did. And I put a lot of effort into my painting, but I always worked with the triumphant feeling that I am an artist, I can do it!

A year later, I held my first exhibition, and over the next few years I painted more than 400 paintings, giving them away to my friends. I held many more personal exhibitions, my paintings are published in magazines, and, most important, I have what makes an artist a true artist, I have my own identity.

The State Institute of Art Studies even asked me to write an article about how an artist can find his own identity.

The author with "A Dancer in March"

Chapter 11.
A Structural Evolutionary-Personal Model of Brainwork

Spirit creates Reality through Nothing.

Hasai Aliev

How Does Thought Become Matter?

Say what you will,
but thought is not matter!
Materialized thought is a metaphor
that refers to its creative power.

Hasai Aliev

I have read many books about how the spirit influences the body, but I have not yet found a clear explanation of how the brain works in this process.

How can simply visualizing a hot iron actually generate a burn, for example?

Or how can visualizing success activate the resources needed to make this a reality?

Saying that it is the subconscious at work means nothing. It is a metaphor that suggests we have valuable stores of information within us which have accumulated over eons of evolution. But how do spirit and matter interact?

We know that visualization helps to achieve the desired goals.

We also know that both visualization and making wise and well-considered decisions require emotional distancing.

This stands to reason, since the fear of making a mistake can arouse stress and interfere with the freedom to think creatively.

As Russian poet Sergei Esenin said, "You cannot see faces when they are up close." The artist does the very same thing when he steps back from his painting every now and again to see how it looks in its entirety.

We also know that the Key creates the emotional distancing necessary for visualization. But how does this help the brain to materialize thoughts and bring about the changes we desire in our lives?

Control of the Dominant State

The world is organized on the basis of interconnecting elements. The higher the level of organization, the greater the number of potential capabilities and possibilities. The human brain is the highest organization of interconnecting elements. A dominant state, as I understand it, is a vector of primarily interneuronic connections, that is, connections between elements.

I will cite the words Academician Alexei Ukhtomsky wrote in his article called "Dominanta i integralny obraz" (The Dominant and the Integral Image) in 1924. He said that in order to have control over human experience, control over yourself and others, and guide human behavior and life itself in a certain direction, you need to control the physiological dominant states in yourself and those around you.

In the physiological language of Academician Ivan Pavlov, a dominant is a site of cortical excitability, that is, highly vigorous activity capable of arresting less vigorous activities.

These definitions are essentially one and the same.

Pavlov showed how a dominant works using the example of how a mother invariably wakes up as soon as her baby starts to cry. This, according to Pavlov, is the watchdog, i.e. the dominant, being activated in the brain.

But how can we create new connections?

Do you know how often you have to repeat something in order to create new connections in the brain?

For example, how often do you have to set your alarm clock in order to wake up at a certain time?

From the new model of brainwork, you will find out what this depends on and that new connections can be formed in specific conditions without any repetition.

For example, a mother lost her son during the terrorist act in Beslan, and a dominant instantly formed, a new connection was created between the two hemispheres of her brain.

Now she thinks about only one thing, that she had a son, and now she does not have a son.

This happened because at the tragic moment both hemispheres of the brain began working synchronously in the same direction, and this unanimity of thought and feeling created a new dominant which a psychologist will have trouble breaking through if he does not have the Key.

And now you will see how ingeniously simply the brain, nature's greatest creation with its incredible capabilities, works.

The brain, as it turns out, works like a simple gear box in a car. The main cerebral shifts occur through the neutral state in which the two hemispheres of the brain become disengaged and are in a state of heightened readiness for new connections, depending on the command.

You can give any command to your inner resources with the help of the Key. But how does the brain work in this way?

And why is the human brain creative?

Gaps in Science about the Brain

If we can figure out how mental and physical inner resources are activated in emergencies, we can learn how to manage these resources.

Contemporary psychological literature points out, for example, that in addition to a state of wakefulness, sleep, and sleep accompanied by dreams, there is also a particular altered state of consciousness (trance) through which, it is believed, resources are activated.

Whereby the term "altered state of consciousness" is not a scientific concept, since alcoholic intoxication or any other similar condition are also called altered states of consciousness.

The well-known theory of the functional systems by Academic Peter Anokhin who, even before Robert Wiener, the author of cybernetics, described the principle of feedback, presupposes that the brain is capable of forming functional systems—work tools—when trying to resolve a problem.

So where does stress come from?

I think it is important to mention the role of psychological or physiological blocks in the origin of stress—the brain may become blocked by fear, complexes, stereotypical thinking, or even physical disorders.

These blocks, like grit in the bearings, impede the restructuring processes in the brain and can cause a rise in uncontrollable neuropsychic tension, i.e. stress.

ATTENTION!

Positive mobilized tension may also create blocks.

For example, an athlete has been training for a competition and visualizing his performance. When his turn came, he made a supreme effort and broke his record. During mobilization of his forces, the required interneuronic connections—a dominant—formed in his brain. But later, once the competition was over, as he calmed down and returned to his normal routine, this dominant continued to work, without becoming integrated into the entire reorganization of the brain's activity. The athlete began having dreams in which he was continuously in a state of anxiety, training for something. For no reason, it seemed, he was unable to relax and return to normal.

In my model of brainwork, I also envisage the formation of post-traumatic syndrome, a similar phenomenon, in which an initially positive mobilizing defense reaction created to combat the stress factor remains active after the event is over and the tension has dissipated and causes a breakdown in the integrity of the brain's restructuring processes.

This description differs from the customary ideas about the development of psychic traumas as a negative aftereffect reaction.

In my model, I supplement the existing models of brainwork with the adaptive mechanism of Discharge-Recharge. This phenomenon is an important part of the overall natural adaptive mechanism called homeostasis, which has been developed by evolution and is activated in each person automatically.

The gist of this mechanism is that switching from minus, negative thinking, to plus, positive thinking, can only occur through zero, the neutral state of brainwork that has never been described before in science.

This mechanism releases the brain from the arrested state caused by blocks and, in so doing, promotes health and creative thinking.

In this sense, the Key helps to release the brain from blocks and ensures more reliable functioning of this mechanism.

The well-known scientific theories contain no descriptions of the structural, essential differences between the basic states of brainwork—the state of wakefulness, sleep, sleep accompanied by dreams, and trance.

These theories also fail to indicate that the interconnection between the two hemispheres of the brain in these different states varies, nor do they provide a description of this system.

So it is difficult to understand how the mechanisms of brainwork change in the different basic states. For example, how do the brain's mechanisms work in the state of wakefulness, the state of sleep, and the state of trance?

And what is the essential, structural foundation of these basic states, which I call aggregate states like the different structural states of water (liquid, ice, and steam).

And how many dominants can function in the brain at the same time, or is there always only one?

What brain model provides an answer to these questions?

A New Model of Brainwork

In a state of free consciousness, there are no fears, complexes, or stereotypes, so the world is perceived in its integrity.
In this state, there is no haste, and we are capable of perceiving specific things while thinking about the eternal from the heights of the loftiest values.
This is probably what it means to know God—when we perceive the the Universe as a single whole and our unique part in it .

Hasai Aliev

The new model of brainwork has been created at the place where psychology, physiology, medicine, biocybernetics, and cybernetics meet and has been confirmed by the results of practical application of the techniques based on it for quickly removing stress, raising stress resistance, and learning self-control and self-management in difficult situations.

I formulated the new model of brainwork in simple and understandable terms so that people from the most diverse fields of specialization can understand each other better when working on such important problems as health, creativity, and longevity.

Science has not yet known such a precisely formulated general theoretical systemic model, and I am proud of the fact that it enhances the development of the Russian psychological and physiological school of thought and is free from any mystical allusions.

This model is the first to describe the essential structural foundation of brainwork, without the multitude of secondary diverse manifestations that prevent researchers from providing constructive answers to such global questions as: how is man structured, how can we raise our resistance to stress, and why is the brain creative?

In the new model, brainwork is described as the interaction between its two functioning hemispheres, whereby one of them is more responsible for information processes, while the other is more connected with energy processes, particularly with emotions and with the body as a whole.

A dominant is formed when both cerebral hemispheres interact synchronously in the same direction. This is what is required for forming new connections of the functional system.

Figuratively speaking, when information interacts with energy, a new reality forms in this communion between thoughts and feelings.

There are five basic states in the new model of brainwork, and each of them has its own way of forming connections between the functional hemispheres of the brain:

1. the state of wakefulness;
2. the state of sleep;
3. the state of sleep accompanied by dreams;
4. the state of trance;
5. the transitional neutral state between these basic states.

In the context of the Key Method, I describe only three states: the state of wakefulness, the state of trance, and the neutral state, which acts as a transition between the indicated basic states.

The State of Wakefulness

**Simultaneous activity between competing dominants
is the structural basis of the state of wakefulness.**

In this state, a multitude of vital connections between the two hemispheres of the brain function at the same time.

This level of activity, which I call semi-dominant organization of brain activity, allows the mind to think and the body to preserve its internal physiological balance regardless of this thinking process.

What does this mean?

At the level of the psyche, which is the foundation of the consciousness, it looks as follows.

The existence of a multitude of simultaneously coexisting competing dominants is precisely the "democracy" that gives people the freedom to make their own decisions, since if there were only one dominant, it would determine all the decisions.

So when there is a multitude of coexisting dominants, our attention is free and mobile.

The attention, i.e. its ability to shift back and forth, is connected with the thought processes.

In physiological terms, the mental cognitive processes and the attention shifts associated with them are accompanied by scanning of the connections between the two hemispheres of the brain.

Thinking is directed toward understanding the meaning, that is, establishing a connection between cause and effect at the highest value level by determining the place of new information in the integrated picture of the world a person has already formed. When this integrated picture of the world is rearranged at a new level, it essentially means that the person has resolved his contradictions, that is, he or she has found a solution to the problem bothering him.

Physiological scanning of the connections between the hemispheres of the brain that occurs during thinking extracts the information and experience from the brain's depositories required for forming the functional systems necessary for solving problems.

The frequency of scanning depends on the level of tension, which, in turn, maintains it and depends on the difficulty of the problem and the supply of reserves. The bigger the problem and the fewer the initial reserves, the higher the tension ensuring the necessary increase in frequency of scanning.

When mental or physical blocks interfere with scanning, the body is enlisted to help.

In so doing, repetitive movements are also activated, for example, gesticulations, while the body may begin to shudder, like a drill trying to penetrate a hard surface, which is manifested in the form of nervous jitters, a tremor, or other phenomena.

The frequency of the repetitive action is dictated by the frequency at which tension and relaxation alternates. These processes of excitability and arrest are a manifestation of the two hemispheres of the brain connecting and disconnecting, via which the brain's depositories are scanned to find the information necessary for resolving the problem.

During disconnecting, discharge occurs, while during connecting, new functional systems are created for solving problems or processing psychological traumas.

This disconnecting and connecting of the two hemispheres of the brain pulverizes problems.

So by helping the scanning process by means of repetitive movements that resonate with the frequency of the shuddering, that is, with the help of the Key techniques, we free the solution-seeking mechanism from its block and are able to find the best solution to the problem.

At the level of psychophysiology, it is precisely the competition among dominants that makes it possible not only to think, but also protects the body from the impact of the mental cognitive processes.

For example, there may be all kinds of different thoughts going on in your head, but this does not prevent your body from functioning normally. Your heart beats steadily and your breathing is even.

Competition among dominants is an integral part of the body's homeostasis mechanism developed by evolution to maintain inner equilibrium during changing conditions. It is due to the simultaneous coexistence of many dominants that we are able to think in different directions, since the competing dominants mutually neutralize each other's impact on the physiological processes. Otherwise, the body would constantly be changing depending on our thoughts.

What is more, the body's autonomy, its independence of the mental processes, makes it possible for us to think freely.

Otherwise, imagine what it would be like if our thoughts about warm weather evoked a feeling of warmth in the body, and thoughts about swimming in a pool changed our breathing and lowered our body temperature. This would interfere with our freedom to think.

So competition among dominants is an integral part of the body's self-regulating mechanism, homeostasis, developed over millions of years of evolution to maintain free consciousness and inner equilibrium during changing conditions.

But as soon as you start thinking about something that arouses strong emotions in you, for example, you imagine how thirsty you are in the heat and how you long for a drink of cold water, everything inside you changes. This is because the activity of both cerebral hemispheres is synchronized in the same direction. The activated dominant becomes stronger, it blocks off the others, and at some point reaches a critical level when all the other dominants are switched off and only this one remains.

Your state has structurally changed, you are in a trance.

And nothing can arrest the body's reflex actions that are aroused in response to the image of the heat and a drink of cold water.

The Trance State

Consecutive activity of the dominants is the structural basis of the trance state.

Trance is a state when only one dominant is active at each consecutive moment. There is only one functional connection between the hemispheres of the brain.

I call this state mono-dominant organization of the brain's activity.

In this state, a person is deprived of the ability to think.

The attention is frozen under the influence of the dominant.

This is the optimal state for bringing decisions and mental commands to fruition. This state ensures one-track activation of the internal organs and body systems, which is manifested as the engagement of internal resources.

A typical example of the trance state is when the concentration is fixed totally on the problem at hand while all competing signals are switched off.

By its very nature, stress is an uncontrolled trance.

When a person experiences stress, his or her attention is focused on the emotionally disturbing situation causing this stress.

When in a trance, the person is hung up on a particular problem. The brain, like a computer that has frozen, does not react to signals that are not part of the dominant focus.

This is why internal reserves can often be engaged in emergencies. In a trance state, in contrast to a state of wakefulness, targeted coordination of the mental and physiological processes occurs under the control of the dominant focus.

In a state of wakefulness, on the contrary, the simultaneous activity of many competing dominants prevents the formation of a dominant state.

I give the following classic example during my lectures.

You are standing in front of a fence and thinking, can I jump over it?

Then you find a malicious dog hot on your heels and you are over that fence in a jiffy!

The survival instinct pushed out all doubts, switching the brain from simultaneous activity of the dominants to their consecutive activity—trance, after adjusting all the processes in the hierarchal chain.

Afterwards, you will probably be amazed at yourself, how could I have jumped over such a high fence?

You were in a trance.

In a state of acute stress, the active stress dominant may block the formation of the psychotherapeutic or target-oriented dominant, since the semantic content of a psychotherapeutic command may contradict the content of the person's stress experiences.

The problem can be resolved by using the Key's ideomotor techniques, since the ideomotor dominant that appears in so doing (which does not have a semantic content) forms automatically, bypassing the person's stress experiences, and, by competing with the stress dominant, neutralizes its potency.

Returning to Beslan…

The mother who lost her son after the terrorist act in Beslan was in a state of acute stress for three days and did not react to the attempts of a psychologist to make verbal contact.

What do psychologists usually do in this case?

Based on the new model of brainwork, we can answer this question; psychologists usually try to activate at least one more dominant focus in the brain that will compete with the active dominant, thus reducing its potency. This is usually achieved by asking the patient to recall some other significant event or positive emotional experience, a childhood memory, for example. Body-oriented psychotherapy techniques, relaxation massage, or similar practices may also be used as additional stress-reducing factors in these cases.

But what if the victim speaks a different language, or is of a different faith? Or what if we are dealing with a child?

How can a psychologist pick the right words to activate the dominant focus and thus remove stress?

Instead of trying to activate the existing dominant, it is much easier to remove stress by creating a new dominant with the help of the Key.

I asked the woman to stand up and simply rock back and forth.

I said that when we were little, our mother held us in her arms and rocked us, and we calmed down, but now we are big and mother cannot pick us up any more, so we have to rock ourselves.

She agreed to try it; this exercise required no effort on her part.

When after about five minutes her body movements became automatic, which showed her tension was being released, signs of Discharge also emerged, she began crying, after which she breathed a sigh of relief and said, "I feel better! What a relief!"

After this, the psychologist was able to establish verbal contact with her and carry out psychotherapy.

All of this took about one hour and brought about a dramatic positive change in how the patient was feeling, the improvement in her frame of mind could be seen right before the eyes. The next day, she went back to work, but she continued with the therapy for another week, one hour every day.

The Neutral State

The absence of a dominant is the structural foundation of the neutral state.

The cerebral hemispheres are functionally discharged, and all temporary connections have been switched off.

This is the psychophysiological basis of emotional distancing.

Only the deep-seated permanent brain connections are retained that were formed during evolution, passed on to you genetically, and serve the body's physiology.

The neutral state, when all dominants are switched off, is naturally activated in life when switching from one brain mode to another, from the state of wakefulness to the state of sleep, and vice versa, from wakefulness to trance, or from sleep to trance, and so on.

This neutral state can be activated both naturally and as a defense reaction at the peak of neuropsychic or physical tension, or, vice versa, at the point of maximum relaxation.

Remember how at times of immense physical exertion, things are difficult at first, but at some point, like a miracle, a feeling of unusually pleasant relief emerges and the work becomes easy. This is called warming to the task or adaptation.

For example, you are running, pushing yourself as fast as you can go, and suddenly you feel lightness, and now you can run without the usual tension and fatigue, your movements require no effort, they become almost automatic.

And your head feels totally empty.

This is usually called getting your second wind.

But second wind actually has nothing to do with it.

Internal resources have been activated because the two hemispheres of the brain begin working synchronously in the same direction. In conditions of extreme tension, when a runner must mobilize his attention and strength to the utmost to perform the next movement, his thoughts and actions come into communion. This is the condition required for coordinating the mental and physical processes.

The ideomotor Key techniques are based on this same communion between thought and action, generating the formation of an ideomotor dominant.

The dominant of running has formed in the runner, ensuring coordination of the body's systems in a single direction that serves the action of running.

Until that moment he was dealing not only with the exertion required to run, but also with psychological blocks, uncomfortable sensations in the body, and doubts about the possibility of winning.

Via the neutral state that appeared at the peak of tension, a switch occurred from the state of wakefulness, where a multitude of dominants reigns, to the trance state, where only one dominant guides all the processes—the dominant that serves the action of running.

Switching off internal contradictions in the mind and body arouses a feeling of lightness.

So it becomes clear that getting one's second wind is secondary, it is a merely a consequence.

When the body's systems are in internal harmony, breathing becomes extremely easy.

This model of brainwork explains the true mechanism of action and so-called holotropic breathwork; it is simply a runner lying on his back.

Why, you may ask, is the customary phenomenon of second wind a consequence of the feeling of lightness that emerges and not the reason for it?

I'll tell you why.

The same feeling of lightness that emerges at the peak of physical exertion or nervous tension also emerges at times of deep relaxation.

For example, in autogenic training a person tries to relax by focusing his attention on a feeling of warmth and heaviness in the body, but when relaxation is achieved, he feels neither warmth nor heaviness, but a feeling of incredible lightness, soaring.

Based on my model of brainwork, it can be understood that through the neutral state, via which the basic states of the brain switch from one mode to another, coordination of the mental and physiological processes occurs: for example, when dozing off—in order to sleep, when running—in order to run, during autogenic training—in order to achieve a state of relaxation and restoration.

With the help of the Key, you can activate the neutral state without lying in bed, anticipating sleep, without running, and without relaxation in comfortable conditions.

You can do it at any time, even while standing on one leg or working on some task.

And the task you are engaged in will become easier, more harmonious, more successful.

Remember the marathon trainer who said that the main thing was to find the right running pace?

With the help of the Key, by bringing your inner processes into communion, you are adapting your body to any activity.

Here it is worth recalling the abovementioned example of helping the woman after the terrorist act.

When I asked her what she felt and what she was thinking about as her body was swaying automatically, she replied, "Nothing. My head was empty."

From the physiological viewpoint, in the neutral state, the temporary flexible connections are disconnected, while the permanent connections between the hemispheres of the brain which control the physiological functions are constantly functioning.

In so doing, the inborn mechanism by which we control our bodies is free from the tension of the negative influence of the temporary connections. In this mode, intensive rehabilitation occurs—restoration of the exhausted and destroyed functions of the body. Everything falls back into place.

From the psychological viewpoint, the neutral state is a state of free consciousness, since it is free from any content. There are no fears, complexes, or stereotypes.

If traces of intense previous mental activity do indeed surface, these thoughts pass freely through the mind without emotional accompaniment, since both hemispheres, the "information-related" and the "energy-related," are disengaged.

> **Repeating mantras and prayers, just like the instinctive swinging of the leg, has a freeing effect that reduces stress and generates a neutral state. While the content of the mantra or prayer is the recharging process that follows this discharge, bringing the inner processes into communion with what is expected from saying the prayer.**

By repeating the movements offered by the Key, you quickly learn how to distance yourself emotionally in order to find the best solution to your problems.

Why is this so?

It is because imitation is one of the basic reflexes.

If a baby starts to cry, other babies nearby also begin crying, if you yawn, the people around begin yawning too. People learn on the basis of imitation, repeating after the teacher. We imitate authorities, we train by repeating certain movements. This is how stereotypical thinking forms. Whereas the ability to distance yourself emotionally at the right moment frees your mind of stereotypical thinking in order to make new and ingenious decisions.

But why is the human brain creative?

They say that man is created in God's image.

How can we know, for no one has ever seen God.

God is a creator, so it would seem that God in man is creativity!

But what is the nature of man's divine structure?

Here I will describe the fundamentals of the brain's creative mechanism.

All the stages of human evolution recur in the human embryo.

The human brain is creative because the powerful evolutionary force produced over millions of years of evolution is condensed in a confined material sheath in the deep-seated connections of the human brain.

The genetic experience of all the previous stages of evolution, of all generations, including the experience of our grandmothers and grandfathers, and even further down to fish and molecules, is condensed in these basic "permanent" connections.

And this powerful evolutionary force, the Universe within us, concentrated in the confined space of the brain, needs to be discharged. Discharge can occur either by destroying the connections—degradation of the personality—or by raising the level of organization in the brain—human development.

Creativity is the most important factor of human biosocial development, the foundation of mankind's health and perfection.

It is precisely in creativity that the cherished and intimate act of connecting our personal experience with the experience of our grandmothers and grandfathers occurs, and, through this interaction between the present and the past, a breakthrough to the future is possible.

This creative evolutionary mechanism for maintaining time links throughout evolution is the foundation of the conceptual foresight and planning that distinguishes man from animals, the foundation of intuition.

Consequently, when you are solving some problem, it is best to distance yourself from it in order to find the best solution, that is, free yourself from fears, complexes, and stereotypes. Therefore, when you solve a task in a state of inner freedom, you are able to find the optimal solution by tapping into the experience of all the previous generations.

And now, may I please have your attention!

You are about to find out where the feeling of levitation, lightness, floating, and weightlessness comes from; people who successfully practice mediation, relaxation, autogenic training, and hypnosis are very familiar with these characteristic sensations. In essence, they are based on one and the same state, but on different vectors, depending on the method used to arouse and apply them.

Incidentally, what do you think a person thinks about when under hypnosis?

What will he say if you ask him?

Have you guessed the answer?

Right! He'll say, "Nothing!" Unless, of course, he has been instructed to think about something in particular.

This is why he is like putty in the hands of the hypnotizer, performing any commands he is given like a robot, because the hemispheres of the brain have been functionally disconnected and are interacting between themselves as dictated by the commands given.

For example, a person under hypnosis will not lower his arm after he has been told to raise it, not because he cannot, but because he does not attempt to do this.

To put it simply, he does not want to lower it.

Why? you ask.

The answer is, because he does not care, he is emotionally distanced from what is happening.

So where does the feeling of levitation, lightness, floating, and weightlessness come from?

You should already know the answer to that question based on our model of brainwork.

That's right, because the hemispheres of the brain are functionally disconnected.

In this state, the brain does not analyze the impulses coming from the body, so the person experiences a feeling of weightlessness.

So you see how simply the brain is structured!

It turns out that the feeling of freedom and the feeling of flight and weightlessness are one and the same mechanism.

And the most amazing thing is that learning to control yourself, that is, being free, means learning to disconnect and connect the hemispheres of the brain whenever you need.

Let's Sum Up What We Have Learned

1. In order to remove stress, at least one more dominant must be created and the brain's work switched from the one-track mode to the simultaneous activity of competing dominants.

2. Use of the Key techniques forms an ideomotor dominant—a new connection between the hemispheres of the brain.

This occurs because doing the exercises, in the same way as a strong emotional irritant, arouses synchronous activity of the two hemispheres by concentrating the attention in the same direction.

3. If a person was in a state of stress, i.e. trance, the dominant formed by the Key brings him out of his trance into a state of wakefulness by causing the dominants to compete with each other.

4. If a person was in a state of wakefulness, the dominant formed, by becoming more potent and switching off the other dominants, transfers the person from a state of wakefulness to a controllable trance.

5. In this state of induced trance, the desired changes and mental sets you think up are transformed into physiological dominants which activate targeted mobilization of the body's resource capabilities in keeping with the content of these set objectives.

In Lieu of a Conclusion

The unconditioned connections responsible for interaction between the hemispheres of the brain are a product of human evolution. They contain, in concentrated form, the entire system of connections that have developed over the millions of years of man's biological and psychic existence.

This system allows the body to physiologically regulate its inner environment in changing conditions and is called homeostasis. In the neutral state, when the brain is free from stress and the involuntary commands, fears, complexes, and stereotypes related to it, the mechanisms of homeostasis function freely. This ensures conditions of intensive and rapid restoration of exhausted and destroyed functions of the body and mind. Here, to put it more simply, everything falls into place.

It is being close to "zero," that is, close to a state of mental and physical equilibrium (psychophysiological balance), that allows a person to visualize all kinds of positive changes.

In contrast, when under stress, for example, the attention is not free, it is fixed on the stress dominant.

It is impossible to visualize desirable changes in the neutral state since there is no desire to think, the connections are disengaged.

You should think about the changes you want to make in yourself and in your life when you come close to "zero," when you have already removed your stress and calmed down but have not yet entered the neutral state.

The emotional distancing that occurs using the Key reduces the effect of external irritants (noise, uncomfortable body position, and so on).

Switching off internal competing signals (fears, complexes, stereotypes, as well as physiological blocks, for example, pain) ensures optimal conditions for free thinking.

The neutral state that consequently emerges creates the conditions necessary to activate the body's resource systems in order to achieve the designated goals.

Everything you have been thinking about disappears into this void created by the disconnected cerebral hemispheres and new functional connections are formed between them.

So I have described how the brain works.

Speaking in metaphors, I have told you how Reality arises from Spirit (ideas, aims) through Nothing (the neutral state).

Onward to Clarity!

We ask ourselves how visualizing the changes we want to make in ourselves and in our lives can actually bring about real changes?

In real life, that is, in the outside world, this concept is more understandable. Life's circumstances can have an effect on how you feel, and by changing the way you feel, you can change your circumstances.

The way we perceive life motivates us to act in certain ways, and these actions create life's new reality.

But what about internally, inside our bodies?

How, for example, can an image or thought cause a physical reaction in the body?

How can visualizing Christ hanging on the cross cause stigmata in religious fanatics?

In actual fact, I have already talked about this mechanism before, but now I will describe it from a different angle, and everything will become clear.

The entire genetic experience of previous generations is contained in the hard connections between the hemispheres of the brain, including the defense reactions to particular irritants that have developed over millions of years. They include reactions to changes in body temperature or blood pressure, heart rate or respiratory functions, and so on.

Physiologist Ivan Pavlov called these adaptive automatic reactions, changes in temperature or blood pressure, for example, unconditioned reflexes. (A reflex action is the body's response to stimuli mediated via the reflex arc, or neural pathway.)

When you climb a hill, your breathing automatically quickens and your heart beats faster, or, for example, you automatically blink and, in so doing, you have involuntarily prevented a speck of dust from falling into your eye. You reach out accidentally to a hot iron, but have already managed to pull your hand away, if you hadn't you would have burned your hand.

But how can you generate a burn by thinking about an iron without the iron actually being physically present?

This is where things get interesting!

The image does not create the reaction, because it is a signal, information; it does not have the necessary energy, it cannot have a real impact on the physical body.

Thought is not matter. Thought, an image, activates a response. A thought stimulates a response if it is potentially programmed in the body when it interacts with a corresponding real factor, an irritant.

A burn is not simply a burn, but the body's defense burn program developed by evolution that is activated when you come in contact with a source of heat with the ensuing neural, biochemical, and other changes.

Pavlov made a distinction between unconditioned reflexes and conditioned reflexes, physical reactions caused by stimuli that reach people in the form of speech, and he called this phenomenon the second signal system.

But when can an image, that is, the virtual model of the real factor, mediate real changes in the body?

Look in front of you at the table.

You see a table.

143

Place your hand on the table.

You feel its surface.

Your eyes have not deceived you, and your fingers confirm this.

It really is a table.

This is how, when the analyzer signal systems (the five sense organs) compete among themselves, the actual existence of an object is established, which arouses a reaction.

And now imagine for a minute that you reach out toward a table and your hand passes through it.

You would most likely experience shock, or at least surprise, what happened?

I will tell you a "secret" about the brain's structure.

If an image, that is a virtual model of reality, is confirmed as reality by competition among the analyzer systems, i.e. its existence is confirmed beyond a doubt, the body will produce a defense reaction, a response programmed by evolution.

If you visualize your hand touching a hot iron, will you actually produce a burn?

I don't think so, unless, of course, you are very suggestible.

But what does suggestibility have to do with anything, what is its mechanism?

Remember again that the signal systems of the brain are competing among themselves and, in so doing, they are confirming the reality of a particular phenomenon.

In other words, when you visualize an iron, you understand that it is only an imaginary iron; so the brain does not produce a programmed response.

What do you need to do for the image to arouse the desired reaction?

The answer is easy, how ingenious everything is!

All you need to do is remove the competition among the analyzer systems!

Either a powerful emotionally disturbing image switches off the competing signals, or you switch off your reaction to the competing signals.

How?

You do this with the help of emotional distancing.

This is the optimal prerequisite for visualization, during which your Ego is also switched off—fears, complexes, and stereotypical thinking, that is, the blocks that stand between the image of the changes you want and the reflexes of your body.

This is how the resources developed during evolution are activated.

The Scriptures say, "According to your faith let it be done to you," or in layman's language, you get what you believe.

This is a metaphor that stirs people into action.

However not every fantasy becomes a reality, no matter how firmly you believe in it, you cannot deceive nature.

But let's talk some more about suggestibility. Now you are familiar with this mechanism.

It is the brain's ability to spontaneously switch off competing signals when focusing attention on an image.

For example, you thought about a dog chasing you and your heart started beating faster, because the dominant formed arrests all the surrounding connections and focuses your attention on the functioning of your internal organs and body systems.

With the help of the Key, you will be able to scale any high fence on your own without a malicious dog on your heels.

When you possess the Key, you can control the dominants in your brain and tap into the experience of past generations to solve your personal problems.

I first published the new model of brainwork in the Russian journals *Innovatsii v obrazovanii* (Innovations in Education), No. 1, 2009 and *Sportivnyy psikholog* (Sports Psychologist), No. 1(16), 2009, and in the books *Otkroi svoi mir! Vkliuchi vnutrenie rezervy* (Discover Your World! Activate Your Internal Reserves), St. Petersburg, Peter Press, 2009, *Le Cle de soi* (Paris, Economica Publishers, 2009), *Silata e v teb! Kliuch k'm sebe si—novite granitsi na cheveshikite v'mozhnosti* (Sophia, Homo Futuris Publishers, 2009). It was published on the Internet for the first time at www.stress.su.

Chapter 12.
Fourteen Questions and Answers

At the seminars I lead, I get asked all kinds of questions, such as: "Can the Key help me to learn a foreign language quicker or become a fast reader?" or "Can the Key help me to meet a girl?", "Will the Key have an effect on my sex drive?" and so on. The answer is the same to all these questions.

And you will know what it is, if you can answer this question: who is more successful, a tense or a relaxed person?

However, people wishing to become acquainted with the Key Method often ask the same questions. Here are a few of the most common ones:

1. How does the method differ from others?
The results come easier and faster.

2. Do you have to do the exercises every day?
When you need to deal with a problem you are having trouble solving, you should do the Synchrogymnastics for 5 minutes every day.

3. Is the sequence you do these five exercises in important?
At first, yes, then you will intuitively know what order to do them in.

4. How can I wave my arms about in public?
If you are out in public and need to use the Key, you can do the exercises in your head, without an audience.

5. How does the method affect the body?
It harmonizes adrenalin and endorphins, reduces the need for oxygen, establishes hormonal balance, regulates your blood pressure, and raises your immunity.

6. How can I cure insomnia using the method?

Use the Twisting exercise from Synchrogymnastics before you go to bed as a Lullaby.

7. How can the method help me to remove nervous agitation?

The first movement is easy: look up at an angle of 45 degrees. Look up with relaxed unfocused and immobile eyes, as though staring into the blue. Blink if you have to. If you wish to close your eyes, go ahead and do so.

Second, sit like that for a minute, letting your thoughts come as they will.

Open your eyes, and you will notice that you have become much calmer.

8. How can the method help me to quit smoking?

At a convenient moment, do the following several times in a row.

For three minutes before using the Key, remember as many unpleasant moments from your life associated with smoking as you can and think again about why you decided to quit smoking.

Concentrate on the fact that just the sight, smell, and smoke of cigarettes nauseates you, causes irritation in your throat, stomach spasms, quickened heart beat and pulse beat in your temples, makes you break out in a cold sweat and feel weak and dizzy.

Then try an exercise that I call The Internal Doctor. This is a very effective way to focus your attention on the problem and reap beneficial results. While standing, relax and concentrate on your most uncomfortable sensations, on the tensest part of your body, or on a spot where you might be feeling pain, and, while focusing your attention in this way, allow your body to do those movements or exercises that arise spontaneously. It is a curative physical exercise that comes from within as prompted by the body. You may find yourself performing the most absurd movements, dancing and gyrating, you may even have a cathartic reaction, such as crying or laughing.

After this exercise, you should sit quietly in the Aftereffect Stage, which reinforces the therapeutic effect and helps to activate the desired changes.

While you do this, visualize how each time you breathe in and out your body is being cleansed, the poison created by cigarettes is being washed away, your anxiety and fear are dissipating, and your lungs are filling with invigorating health-inducing fresh air. This feeling of invigoration and health envelops your entire body, and you become free and confident in yourself.

9. How can the method help me to stop drinking?

Do the following. For three minutes before using the Key, remember as many unpleasant moments from your life associated with alcohol as you can and think again about why you decided to stop drinking.

Concentrate on the fact that just the sight, smell, and taste of alcohol nauseates you, causes irritation in your throat, stomach spasms, quickened heart beat and pulse beat in your temples, makes you break out in a cold sweat and feel weak and dizzy.

Then do The Internal Doctor exercise.

While you do this, visualize how each time you breathe in and out your body is being cleansed, the poison from the alcohol is being washed away, your anxiety and fear are dissipating, and invigorating health-inducing fresh air is filling your every cell. This feeling of invigoration and health envelops your entire body, and you become free and confident in yourself.

You become free and confident in yourself in the way you sometimes felt while under the influence of alcohol, but now you can be free and confident every day without leaning on this crutch. And visualize yourself clearly as you step out lightly, your head held high, full of energy, smiling, and with bright shining eyes.

Think about how you have two different faces, one of them, on the left, is bloated, sagging, and wrinkled, while the other, on the right, is young-looking, animated, and glowing, and between them stands a glass of alcohol. It is just one glass, but that is all it takes to trigger a chain reaction; the choice is yours. Which one is you, the one on the left, or the one on the right?

10. How can the method help me to lose weight?

At a convenient moment, do the following several times in a row.

For three minutes before using the Key, remember as many unpleasant moments from your life associated with eating something you shouldn't, something sweet, for instance.

Concentrate on the fact that just the sight, smell, or taste of this food nauseates you, causes irritation in your throat, stomach spasms, quickened heart beat and pulse beat in your temples, makes you break out in a cold sweat and feel weak and dizzy.

Then do The Internal Doctor exercise.

While you do this, visualize how each time you breathe in and out your body is being cleansed from this "poison," your anxiety and fear are dissipating, and invigorating health-inducing fresh air is filling your every cell. This feeling of invigoration and health envelops your entire body, and you become free and confident in yourself.

Visualize how you want to look, picture all the details of your slender figure, light step, how you stand straight and tall, are full of energy, smiling, and with bright shining eyes.

After this, your body will start prompting you about what to eat, you will want to do exercises, and even your wrinkles will disappear. If your hair has started falling out or become gray because of stress or nutrition imbalances, it will grow back in and return to its natural color.

Example

A woman wishing to lose extra weight went for a blood test to see if she had a food allergy and was given recommendations about what to eat. But as soon as she was under stress, she quit her diet. "When I'm stressed," she said, "I grab a piece of bread and spread butter on it."

She was told that people mainly eat to calm themselves down, chewing also reduces stress, and so if you use the fast-acting Key techniques once or twice a day, the need for food decreases.

"What food could you eat instead of a piece of bread and butter when under stress? And what figure would you like to have as a result?"

"I'm allowed pears, mandarins, meat," she replied.

"Carry a mandarin or pear in your bag, and replace your old stereotype with a new one; when you do the Key techniques think about the figure you would like to have and about how you are going to enjoy eating a pear instead of a piece of bread and butter."

11. How can I regulate pain using the techniques?

There is pain, and there is the personal experience of pain, the suffering that is connected with pain. Using the Key techniques creates emotional distancing, a state in which the personal experience of pain can be switched off.

12. How can I discover my creative potential with the help of the Key?

I can give you my own personal example. While doing the Key techniques, I visualized myself painting only masterpieces, and whenever doubt crept in, I did the tension-releasing exercises. This made me feel confident that I would succeed, and when a person feels this way everything really does work out.

13. Can a child learn the Key method?

When a child is small, you rock him in your arms to calm him down. An older child achieves the same effect when he involuntarily swings his leg or drums his fingers on the desk.

Then he dances rock and roll and does other gyrating movements.

You can teach him some of the Synchrogymnastics exercises he finds easiest to do. This will help him to be less tired and remove tension without swinging his leg.

Even children can learn the easy Key techniques

14. Dear Dr. Aliev! I am amazed! I used the Key in the water. I filled my lungs with air and hung in the water like a float. I used the Key and visualized my body bending to the left. And my body bent to the left. Then I visualized it bending to the right and back. And it bent in the water, obeying my commands, I didn't do anything at all, I only gave my body commands. I showed my father. My father also did the same. What is this?

Commands tell the body muscles what to do, just like when you do the Key techniques and your arms move apart and float up in response to your visualization. You have no doubt heard of flying yogis? Well, while sitting in the Lotus position, they imagine that their bodies leave the ground and levitate. They say, today we will rise 5 centimeters, tomorrow, ten, and the day after tomorrow, we'll fly!

I have studied this phenomenon. It is not flight, but jumps activated by the automatic contraction of the leg muscles in response to how they visualize themselves flying as they meditate.

People who do not know about this phenomenon of muscle contraction simply believe that yogis are really able to fly.

But now they know about it and can discard their misguided thinking to truly develop their own real and boundless capabilities.

Chapter 13.
From Praise to Practical Assessment

I receive a lot of letters from people who have taken my courses or read my books, and I take great pleasure and interest in reading each and every one of them. Of course, some of the messages are very original. For example, a 12-year-old boy wrote: "Send me the Key, I really need it you know!!"

And someone else wrote in an urgent telegram: "Please send me self control, cash on delivery!"

But on a more serious note, here are a few of the reviews I have received.

Oleg Khopersky, head trainer of the Russian yachting team, and Alexei Anikin, the team's physician, write:

In July 2007, a Key anti-stress training session was organized in Portugal for the members of the Russian yachting team. In a very short time, Hasai Aliev managed to rid the team members of their loser syndrome and teach them how to evoke a frame of mind conducive to achieving good results in tough competitive conditions.

The Key techniques also helped the team members learn how to significantly reduce the effect of negative emotions manifested in the form of rapid heartbeat, headaches, a sensation of heaviness in the arms and legs, and so on. During the training, the team members were able to free themselves from thoughts that they were in a stressful situation and form vegetative reactions that helped to raise their level of psychological and psychophysiological stability.

As practice has shown, the Key techniques are particularly effective in reducing the stress-induced reaction to an upcoming stressful event, such as a competition. By following Hasai Aliev's techniques aimed at preparing them for important competitions, the team members were able to create a model of behavior they could use in future stressful situations. For example, they were able to program themselves for success, visualizing their victory over rivals in future competitions, developing and honing the mental skills needed to be a winner, and so on. In other words, they created new stereotypes of behavior to be used in stressful situations in the future. This is how the Key's ideomotor techniques can be used to reinforce new orientations at the psychophysiological level.

We need to continue using the Key method when working with skilled athletes in different sports in order to improve psychological training for major international competitions.

This is what Liudmilla Yurievna, a business women from Moscow, writes:

The method is so simple that the first question you want to ask is, does it really work?

The answer is, yes, it works.

I tried the Synchrogymnastic myself, although only for a few days.

What did I feel?

I began reacting more calmly to things I would normally get irritated or even angry about.

Everything fell into place. It has always been hard for me to make a choice, but after doing the Key exercises I am able to clearly see the choice that suits me best and discard the rest.

I am sure that in the future, by using your Key Method and what I learned at the seminar, I will be able to do everything I set my mind to, and maybe even more.

I feel just great, full of strength and energy.

I received the next letter from Israel:

I have been wanting to write and thank you for your Key Method for several years now, since it has helped me to do a special kind of creative work I really enjoy.

About fifteen years ago when I was still living in Moldavia, I saw a TV program about you where you explained how to enter that wonderful elevated state. I was able to do it the very first time. Since this method helps to achieve inner balance and harmony, it is priceless; it is wonderful and beneficial. I am not a psychologist, or a social worker, it is just important for me personally to be able to enter that special meditative state, that resuscitating Void from which all creation springs, as the ancient Chinese believed. I began drawing in this state with half-closed eyes, my hands barely coming in contact with the desk, the felt-tip pen hardly touching the paper, as though my hand were moving over smooth water, lightly caressing the surface....the lines I draw are smooth, and images appear without any preliminary thought. I do not actually see in my mind's eye what I want to draw, I just think up a topic. I have no idea where the images come from, either from the depths of my subconscious, or from some independent data bank, from the Void. But the drawings turn out differently from what I might draw in my customary tense state. They are very dear to me! I only think up the topic, I do not see the picture I want to draw and I do not know where my hand holding the pen will take me, it is as though it is not me drawing at that moment, but someone is guiding my hand.

I have been living in Israel for 14 years now, and despite all the high-strung emotions and anxiety in this part of the world, people live by their creative interests. Only goodwill, an interest in different cultures, and an attempt to realize your own creative potential make it possible to rise above our brutal and mercantile world. Your method helps me to stay afloat, be part of nature and a unique individual element of it.

And this is what one of my students who asked to remain anonymous writes:

I began practicing the principles of your method as early as 1992, before I knew you and the scientific-medical research you are engaged in. For more than three years, almost every day, I entered an altered state of consciousness and permitted my body to be in free flight, while giving my body organs and systems commands designed to achieve self control. Then I went on to self-teaching, massage, acupuncture, and energy passes.

In this way, I dealt with many psychosomatic problems and began to control many psychophysiological processes. What is more, an information channel opened up within me and I was able to see the intricate structures of the human body; in this state I began to write poetry. This all went on to pave the way to further self-awareness...

These are the impressions of only a few trainees for whom the Key Method became the beginning of a new higher-quality life.

Dr. Hasai Aliev

I hope that you too will find my book elucidating and helpful.

So that you can make a note of the results you achieve from doing the exercises and of the positive changes that occur in your life, there is space at the end of the book for you to write down your own aims, how quickly you achieve them, and your impressions. I wish you good health and long years of creative endeavor!

Assessment of the Key Method's Effectiveness

The many letters I have received from people who have been using the Method to solve different problems, as well as my daily work with patients and students, describe the benefits and advantages of the Key Method.

For those who prefer to put their trust in more objective tests, I can assure you that many scientific investigations have been done in different parts of Russia to assess the Method's effectiveness and efficiency.

Since scientific tests are usually complicated in terms of their contents and methodology, I have chosen to briefly describe the investigations that were carried out and the conclusions that were drawn.

Three surveys were carried out to assess the method's effectiveness:

1. Survey of the effect on the coefficients of fatigue, performance efficiency, and physical endurance (those surveyed included microassembly operators, athletes, a group of volunteers—a total of 440 people).

2. Survey of the method's efficiency during anti-stress training of people engaged in dangerous professions (a total of 656 people).

3. Evaluation of the effectiveness of the Key techniques during emergency rehabilitation of terrorist act victims (2,500 people).

Total number of people surveyed—3,596.

A set of psychological and psychophysiological methods was used to assess the effectiveness of the method, including:
- structured interviews;

- self-report inventories of those surveyed on their wellbeing;
- visual monitoring of the dynamics of the physical condition of terrorist act victims;
- monitoring of the dynamics of arterial blood pressure and heart rate.

In order to make monitoring of the changes and data obtained objective, each person's mental wellbeing was assessed at the beginning and at the end of entire session.

The surveys were carried out both in laboratory conditions and in real conditions of anti-stress training of people engaged in dangerous professions and rendering medical and psychological assistance to victims of terrorist acts.

Conclusions

1. The Key Method based on guided ideomotor techniques makes it possible to raise the level of stress resistance, develop skills of psychophysiological self-control, reduce the training time, ensure the possibility of developing skills in conditions close to reality, lower the level of stress in extreme situations, and speed up restoration of psychophysiological wellbeing.

2. It has been established that use of the Key Method makes it possible to reduce the intensity of stress reactions and reliably improve hemodynamic and angiotonic parameters of blood circulation.

3. Use of the Key Method makes it possible to significantly improve the coefficients of physical and operative performance efficiency (the Harvard Step Test by 10%, sensorimotor reaction by 10%, and the integral wellbeing/activity/mood coefficient by 24%).

4. The Key Method is much faster than traditional methods for producing the desired results and does not require any special facilities or conditions for doing the exercises. Restoration of psychophysiological wellbeing is achieved 1.5-3-fold faster.

5. The Key Method is the method of choice for people who have demanding jobs, athletes, people engaged in dangerous professions, and victims in need of rapid rehabilitation, as well as for training a large number of people at once in stress management skills in conditions where verbal contact is problematic.

Chapter 14.
History of the Method

After I held training sessions in the Key Method in the Netherlands (Molenhoek, 2006), Dutch and German specialists asked how I had managed to create such a simple and fast-acting method.

I said that each culture creates its own methods, this method is a Russian achievement, since Russia is a country where people want to attain instant success without any effort. The method is equally understood by people of the West and the East and could only come into being at the crossroads between the West and the East. The West represents outer values and material freedoms, while the East symbolizes internal, spiritual values. The Key techniques combine exercises that are semi-outward (movements) and semi-inward (reflexes). By uniting the West and the East within myself, I discovered my inner freedom.

At the end of the 1970s, I was working as a reflex therapist in a polyclinic in Makhachkala in Daghestan in the Northern Caucasus. At that time, I was trying to find a synthesis between acupuncture and hypnosis. It was then that I made my first scientific discovery. I discovered a phenomenon previously unknown to science. The response evoked by acupuncture points could be activated without direct physical stimulation.

One day, while conducting a regular therapeutic hypnosis session at my polyclinic, I decided to put an idea that had long been floating around in my head to the test. So while I waited for my patients to become immersed in their hypnotic trance, I handed each of them a felt-tip pen and gave them the following instructions: "You feel energy similar to a weak electric current running up through your body from your toes to your head. Use the felt-tip pen to draw the path this current is taking." And I froze in anticipation, for I was very interested to see what my patients would do. And lo and behold, they began drawing a line that directly traced the meridian lines or channels identified in the Reflexotherapy Atlas. I could hardly believe my eyes; the lines they drew went along the channels that link the reflex points, although my patients had never seen the Atlas. Whereby each patient touched on precisely those points that corresponded to his or her ailment. The patient who had a stomach ulcer, for instance, drew a line through the reflex points that need to be stimulated for treating stomach ulcers, and the patient who suffered from radiculitis marked the points and channels that are usually penetrated by needles when treating radiculitis.

The stimulation that is usually aroused with the help of needles, electric current, massage, laser beam, or other instruments could now be aroused by exclusively targeted hypnotic suggestion, in other words, through the cerebral cortex with the help of an image that forms a model characteristic of its nervous response—the sensation of an electric current.

The Key Method, my second discovery, appeared a little later when Adrian Nikolaev, the planet's third astronaut, asked me to come up with a way that would enable an astronaut to activate an electric current in himself at the necessary points without any hypnosis.

From Weightlessness to a Feeling of Relief

I created the Key Method of guided psychophysiological self-control at the Gagarin Astronaut Training Center in 1981 in order to simulate a state of weightlessness in astronauts on the ground and help them to cope with stress and overload.

I asked the group of astronauts to relax and imagine the state of weightlessness they feel in space.

Their arms began to automatically float up and that special state of inner lightness emerged.

I asked a control group of trainees who did not have any experience with weightlessness to visualize their arms rising into the air.

Their arms automatically floated up, whereby this was accompanied by a feeling of inner lightness and removal of stress, headaches, and fatigue.

So the first basic Key techniques appeared that help us discover our ability to control our inner state.

In 1984, the first extensive practical use of the method was carried out in the electronic industry for reducing visual fatigue in microassembly operators, women working with microscopes.

In 1987, the method was approved by the Soviet Ministry of Public Health and recommended for reducing stress and fatigue in workers, as well as for psychoprophylaxis and treating different neurotic disturbances and psychosomatic illnesses (phobias, anxiety attacks, contextual depression, hypertensive disease, cardiac angina, bronchial asthma, digestive disturbances, osteochondrosis, back pain, early diabetes, and so on).

For its ease of understanding and high effectiveness, the method was awarded a medal at the 2nd International Symposium on Systems Research, Informatics and Cybernetics held in Baden-Baden, West Germany, in 1989.

Since 1989, the method has been used to train dispatchers at energy enterprises in Daghestan, the Northern Caucasus.

At different times, directors of subdivisions of Mosenergo, members of the Club of Directors of Industrial Enterprises of Russia, students of the Russian Academy of National Economy, students of the Tallinn School of Managers founded by Vladimir Tarasov and the Arsenal School of Management in Moscow, distributors of Poland's Amexim Trade Company, hotline operators working at Mondo X, a foundation established by Padre Eligio for treating young people with drug addictions, specialists of children's rehabilitation centers under the Children of Russia presidential program, psychologists of employment centers working with the unemployed in Moscow, Nizhny Novgorod, and Cheboksary, war veterans and veterans of Moscow's Armed Forces, heads of the Silvinit Mining Enterprise in Solikamsk, and test pilots of the international Mars 500 space program have all taken psychological training courses in the Key Method.

Members of the Ararat Armenian football team, the Central Sports Club fencing team, the Anji football team, Moscow's Dinamo hockey team, Nizhny Novgorod's Torpedo hockey team, wrestlers of the Republic of Daghestan, and the Russian yachting team have all taken training courses in the Key Method at different times to activate their inner resources when participating in challenging sports events.

Since 1995, the Key Method has been used as a vital component for treating acute stress in children and adults who were victims of the terrorist acts in Kizlyar, Kaspiisk, Essentukhi, and Beslan.

In 1997, the Stress Management Center Nongovernmental Educational Institution was established in Moscow. Dr. Hasai Aliev is its founder and director, and specialists in 105 Russian and CIS cities, as well as in the U.S., Holland, Germany, Israel, and Canada, have taken his training courses (www.stress.su).

For ten years, psychologists of the Russian Ministry of Internal Affairs and Ministry of Education, rescue squads, and other people working in dangerous and stressful professions who are sent to combat and disaster zones have been participating in anti-stress training sessions based on the Key Method.

This book is an effort within the framework of a new project aimed at establishing the Hasai Aliev International Institute for the Development of Human Capabilities.

Chapter 15.
The Synchromethod Is Free Inner Time

If man is created in God's image, and
God is a creator, it would seem that
God in man is creativity.

Hasai Aliev

We all need free time, and not only time for doing the things we like to do, but, most important, time when we are free from the demands and pressures of the outside world, time when we can turn inward and take care of our own personal needs.

It is important, especially if you live in a big noisy city, to set aside at least five minutes a day when you can be free from the hustle and bustle of everyday life, from the burden of ongoing concerns and worries, and spend some time alone with yourself in a place of inner peace and quiet in order to hear your own inner music amid the cacophony of the general world orchestra and understand what you want and how best to achieve it.

Even if you are exhausted after a long day's work, even if it is very late in the evening, you will be unable to sleep until you have satisfied this natural need for solitude. You will keep going over the emotional points of the day in your head. This is known as discharge. And if you do not allow yourself to discharge, the tension will grow.

You instinctively discharge while sitting in front of the television, for example, switching from channel to channel and thinking your own thoughts while staring blankly at the screen. Or children, for example, who are tired of doing homework, will play computer games that do not require any intellectual effort, or do require it, but in a different way.

Thoughts keep churning over in your head, and as you know now from reading this book, if you try to stop them, your tension will grow. This is a good time to do the Twisting exercise, which helps your thoughts to turn over more easily and to free up your mind.

In quiet solitude, you can calmly think over decisions, whereas when you are under pressure, you are unable to think freely. The main problem in life, and in any training method for that matter, is that you learn or attune yourself while in one situation, whereas you have to apply the knowledge and act in different, including emergency, situations.

For example, in the evening, after everyone has gone to bed and you have time to yourself, you begin thinking about your plans for tomorrow, and everything falls neatly into place, you are able to clearly see what you have to do.

You have thought everything out very well. You have come up with an inspiring strategy for talking to your boss tomorrow, or to your friend, or to a future work partner. And you seem to have covered all your bases. You have been thinking easily and freely about what you will do tomorrow and anticipated the desired result.

But in the morning, when you walk into your office, you are thrown off balance.

The situation is not what you anticipated. There are phones to answer, visitors to see. The person you want to talk to is in a hurry.

In your confusion, you tell him only snatches of your thoughts, and he also answers in snatches.

You are talking, but you are not saying the things you wanted.

You feel stressed. There is no clarity of thought, no mutual understanding. Nothing is working out. You are not in charge of the situation. All you want is to somehow keep your head above water, but you are floundering.

You walk away and only later, when you no longer feel stressed, do you see things clearly again. And you say to yourself, "Oh, I should have said such-and-such. I should have responded in such-and-such a way."

Unfortunately, it is most often the person who is able to keep a cool head and remain calm before the television camera or microphone, for example, who comes out on top and not the person who actually has something important to say. After all, when all the chips are down, instinct comes into play, and the person who can present his case with the most confidence is the one people listen to, because it is obvious that he knows what he is talking about and what to do.

It is even difficult for experienced actors who have learned their part in advance to retain clarity of mind and confidence in themselves in demanding emotional situations, including before the television camera or live audience. Actors are especially taught how to remain calm and collected using a variety of tension-releasing techniques. With the help of the Key, you too can learn how to gain this control over yourself, rid yourself of extraneous thoughts and worries, and free yourself from anxiety.

People have a natural ability to reflect, distance themselves from the world around them, and become immersed in their own thoughts. It is almost an automatic reflex.

No matter what you are doing, working on a project or listening to music, you will always, often without realizing it, tune into yourself for a few seconds or moments.

There are people who are more closely attuned to themselves than others.

There are anxious hypochondriac people who are always looking for something wrong in themselves. Being attuned to yourself is nothing new, it is a human capability, similar to a computer, which when switched on scans itself, checking the condition of its internal systems to make sure they are in good working order.

After a few short sessions using the Key, your life will become easier and richer in content.

You will acquire a feeling of inner protection.

You will continue to tune into yourself. But now, instead of searching for damaged parts, you will be looking for that wonderful state of inner harmony and lightness. Instead of finding things to be anxious about, your introspection will become a tuning fork that guides you toward greater health and wellbeing.

And you will have more free time.

Free Sailing to Health, Happiness, and Success

You are in a bad mood and want to lift your spirits, but you are unable to do it. Remember the Key, do the tension-releasing exercises for a few seconds, they will release inner blocks and you will feel internally free again and be able to think in constructive and positive ways.

Or you need to resolve some very difficult problem, but you just do not seem to be able to achieve a favorable outcome.

Take a break and do something different, spend a few minutes with your favorite Key exercises. They will bring you out of your state of stagnant overtension and you will quickly find a solution to your problem.

Everyone has wish lists, day-dreaming is an inherent part of our nature, but our dreams do not always come true.

And when do dreams come true? When do wishes come to fruition? When there is communion between the mind and the body, when there is inner harmony between the body and the soul.

Visualize the changes you want to make in yourself, in your life, in your character and habits, and in your health using the Key exercises, and your dreams will start coming true. The method brings about changes in your life because what you do depends on your perception of yourself and your life. As you practice the techniques, your perception will improve and this will legitimately lead to actual changes in your life.

I hope that as you find new energy and joy in living with each passing day, and not only from achievements, compliments, or gifts, but also from your new-found feeling of inner harmony and wellbeing, you will also remember me, your counselor. Let this be my living contribution to your health and happiness.

You Are a Person of the Future

I always wondered what people of the future would be like.

Others may wonder what new technology, cars, spacecraft, the future holds in store, but I always wondered what new qualities and capabilities people of the future would have.

And I always felt sad that I personally would not live to see the day.

But once when I happened to be thinking about this as I was doing the Key exercises, I suddenly saw the truth!

The people of the future will be the same as us, only they will outshine us and be happier and healthier than us, because they will be better able to manage their inner state.

After I realized this truth, I calmed down once and for all. It was as though something had clicked between me and them, the people of the future, some internal time link had been established, as though the people of the future and I were now one.

And now I feel as though I am immortal.

Each of us is a person of the future, and our task is to discover ourselves.

Appendix A:
My Personal Success Diary

What do I expect from the Key?

_____

_____

_____

_____

_____

_____

What is my problem? (date)

_____

_____

_____

_____

_____

_____

1st day of exercises:
How do I feel before discharge?
(stress scale: 0 = calm – 10 = very stressed)

_____

_____

_____

_____

_____

_____

How do I feel after discharge?
(stress scale: 0 = calm – 10 = very stressed)

_____

_____

_____

_____

_____

What exercises did I do well, and what interfered?

_____

_____

_____

_____

_____

The positive changes I have noticed:

_____

_____

_____

_____

2nd day of exercises:
How do I feel before doing the exercises?

_____

_____

_____

_____

_____

How do I feel after doing the exercises?

_____

_____

_____

_____

_____

The positive changes I have noticed:

_____

_____

_____

_____

_____

3rd day of exercises:
How do I feel before doing the exercises?

_____

_____

_____

_____

_____

How do I feel after doing the exercises?

_____

_____

_____

_____

_____

The positive changes I have noticed:

_____

_____

_____

_____

_____

4th day of exercises:
How do I feel before doing the exercises?

_____

_____

_____

_____

_____

_____

How do I feel after doing the exercises?

_____

_____

_____

_____

_____

_____

The positive changes I have noticed:

_____

_____

_____

_____

_____

_____

5th day of exercises:
How do I feel before doing the exercises?

_____

_____

_____

_____

_____

_____

How do I feel after doing the exercises?

_____

_____

_____

_____

_____

_____

The positive changes I have noticed:

_____

_____

_____

_____

_____

_____

10th day of exercises:
What is my problem today?

_____

_____

_____

_____

_____

_____

How do I feel compared to the 1st day of exercises?

_____

_____

_____

_____

_____

What has changed for the better in me and in my life?

_____

_____

_____

_____

_____

_____

I am raising my goals!
What else do I want to change or achieve in my life? How do I see
myself in the future?

_____

_____

_____

_____

_____

_____

20th day of exercises:
What is my problem today?

_____

_____

_____

_____

_____

How do I feel compared to the 1st day of exercises?

_____

_____

_____

_____

_____

What has changed for the better in me and in my life?

_____

_____

_____

_____

_____

_____

What else do I want to change or achieve in my life? How do I see myself in the future?

_____

_____

_____

_____

_____

_____

30th day of exercises:
What is my problem today?

_____

_____

_____

_____

_____

How do I feel compared to the 1st day of exercises?

_____

_____

_____

_____

_____

What has changed for the better in me and in my life?

_____

_____

_____

_____

_____

I am raising my goals even higher!
What else do I want to change or achieve in my life? How do I see myself in the future?

_____

_____

_____

_____

_____

Appendix B:
A Novella by Hasai Aliev

> *We are all capable of creating a masterpiece,*
> *Because people cannot live without ideals.*
> *So if you are feeling down, if the world seems gray,*
> *If you are finding fault with everyone around you,*
> *it means that at that moment you are not creating.*
> Hasai Aliev

Anguish Over a Spoiled Painting

Every artist knows this feeling, he wants to make his paintings better and better, and...

But here I would also like to talk about something else.

Once I became very interested in finding out what high artistic elite creativity was all about.

Everyone talks about high culture, the appreciation of what is sometimes referred to as High Art. They look long and hard at paintings, evaluate and appreciate them.

They are connoisseurs of high art!

I remember how in school we went on a trip to a museum. Everyone looked attentively at the paintings, sighed, and whispered, wonderful, magnificent, great works!

But I stood there without a clue and wondered what it was they saw that was so wonderful?!

I knew my school friends very well, a bunch of nitwits, so I was surprised they were able to see something of particular value in the paintings. High art indeed! Just like me, they probably did not see anything, it was just their monkey instinct responding.

Of course, even if you cannot sing, you can still catch a wrong note when you hear it. There is harmony in each and every one of us, that extraordinary universal sense of hearing—a feeling of harmony, an instinct for the truth.

But can you really appreciate a high achievement and become enthused over a masterpiece if you have never tried doing something similar yourself? Try it. Pick up a brush and paint the sunshine!

I never thought I could draw.

In school, we were given an apple or a hammer and told to draw it.

But I never could.

I couldn't even draw a straight line.

So I thought I didn't know how to draw.

Petrov over there is an artist, but not me.

As an adult, I saw paintings that were out of the ordinary, impetuous, without straight, neat lines, with thick layers of different colors. They were nothing like the paintings I had seen before, they sparked my interest and filled me with wonder.

So that's how you can paint if you want to!

And I could paint like that! And it turned out that theses paintings were also of high artistic value.

When you find out that what you can and know how to do has value, you want to do it, you want to work! Success kindles faith in yourself.

This was my first revelation.

The second revelation I owe to my friend Rakhman, the artist, who said that painting is euphoria.

I had never heard such a definition of creativity before. So creativity can arouse euphoria, I thought to myself.

People usually talk about how creativity requires a lot of effort, a creative person has a hard road to hoe.

And this puts people off searching for freedom.

It smacks of keeping people in chains and slave mentality.

But painting can be euphoric!

My artist friend painted while he walked back and forth singing to himself.

And when I too started to paint, I began to understand, the truth was revealed, so to speak.

And it turns out that the truth is revealed through recognizing the effort required to achieve it. Conscious labor is what euphoria is all about. Then you are able to see the fruits of your labor.

Feeling the joys and pains of working on a painting, working now in one mood, now in another, and seeing how these moods, colors, the size of the canvas, and everything on earth influence the painting, I was able to understand that there is nothing coincidental in this world.

I realized that every joyous unique stroke contains a wealth of emotions and lives a life of its own; it reflects your health, your doubts, your belief in the truth of your ideas, and your belief in yourself. Now I was able to understand that a masterpiece is created not through the skillful mixing of colors, but through the concentration of every human effort, through the victory of spirit.

They say my paintings are good, they have meaning. Others are told that their paintings are like Picasso's, Chagall's, or Van Gogh's …

It makes me happy when I hear that I am unique … that I have my own identity.

And I still can't draw a hammer. But who cares!

In the very beginning, when I had only just started painting, in those very early days, I immediately discovered three things that are necessary to create a work of art.

Even though my artist friend Rakhman said that there would be a million more such discoveries, that I would discover something new in my painting every time, I discovered these three things straight away.

First, every painting, or at least one spot in it, should hold a mystery.

Then the meaning of the entire painting reveals itself, like in a fairytale.

Second, in order to do this, all the colors used in the painting should be concentrated in that spot; just like a fistful of earth contains almost the whole of Mendeleev's periodic table of elements.

And third… the meaning itself.

The artist, of course, is not the one who paints a painting, but the one who expresses meaning in the language of painting.

Abstractionists, modernists, avant-garde painters…

Character can be expressed with one brush stroke. But some need more dots to be able to see the connection, they need realism, while others even need….photographs.

I do not like abstractionists, modernists, and avant-garde painters. They are searching, at the experimental stage, attempting to reach the heights.

An artist is someone who, having reached the abstract heights, comes back down to earth, to real life.

Eastern philosophy says that for the person who has not experienced satori (enlightenment), a stream is just a stream, mountains are just mountains, a forest is just a forest.

However, for the person who has experienced satori, the enlightened one, mountains are again mountains, a stream is a stream, and a forest is a forest.

The greatest height of perception is life itself. The same applies to poetry. As literary editor Yakov Chernyak once said, "Despite his complexity, Pasternak allegedly demonstrated a 'Pushkinian clarity'."

Speaking of clarity...

I painted furiously...every night until six in the morning, with complete abandon. So from the very first attempt my paintings were unlike anything else. (This is not for the critics, critics will find the amateur in them, but still they are unlike anything else.) I had no teaching, only passion...and life experience. And I lived in the belief that everything living is priceless.

And I was so inspired! I became extremely carried away.

And for me, someone with no skills, it was amazing how one painting followed another.

I was covered from head to foot in paint.

Did I drink coffee? Yes!

Did I sleep? I suffered from a chronic lack of it.

Did I smoke too much? Yes!

Did I go and see my friends afterwards? You bet I did!

Did I drink beer? For several days in a row.

I sat with a friend, a government minister, and we talked about how the central government, the country's Center, should represent all the cultures of the nations, like all the colors on a canvas.

This is what the Center and the provinces is all about.

What else can politics be about?

Then the Center will respect the provinces, and the provinces will respect the Center.

Was it an accident that my friend placed a piece of bread on top of the glass?

I sat and looked at that glass with the bread sitting on top.

That could be the subject of my next painting, I thought; a large cut glass tumbler filling the entire canvas with a piece of bread on top.

"I'll give you that painting!" I told my friend later.

And again I painted all night...until six in the morning.

I started painting over a canvas I had almost finished. It was a magnificent desert done in bright yellows and dazzling reds, conveying the intense heat of the wind, glowing and vibrant. It was a masterpiece.

180

But in my drunken state, blues and blacks began appearing on the canvas as I tried to paint the glass on the desert sands. It was just not turning out, and the piece of rye bread sitting atop the glass was not turning out, everything was turning a swamp green, and I too was covered in swamp green paint.

And at six in the morning, when I went to bed, my blood pressure had risen.

I closed my eyes and saw a canvas before me.

And depending on my thoughts, the painting instantaneously changed before my eyes, and everything was so harmonious, masterpieces were created in an instant.

There was a green dot, and on it a perfect black shadow, just as it should be, or suddenly a blue corner appeared, and on it a darker blue dip, and the bread did not appear as I had tried to draw it, but just as it was supposed to look, like natural rye, and the glass under it was not the way I had drawn it, but just right, drawn at an angle.

And this went on all night. Everything I thought of appeared on the painting before my eyes, and each moment everything changed. My brain was broiling. It was as though I immediately saw how I was supposed to draw. It was as though I had stepped over some hurdle.

Now I was an artist!

But it was sort of frightening. I just could not fall asleep. My brain was churning.

I remembered this later and analyzed it.

Nothing is coincidental.

There have been three extraordinary similar instances in my life.

Once I was typing for a long time on a typewriter, for a few days and nights in a row, and after I had finished it was as though I could not stop. Everything I thought about appeared before my eyes as though I were typing it on a piece of paper. My exhaustion was producing these obsessive thoughts.

Here is another example.

I went to visit some border guard friends. They took me fishing.

We fished all day in the sun. I sat looking at the float...

The float stood quietly in the water, bobbing up and down, for a long, long time. Then suddenly, it jerked, up and down, then it disappeared under the water. Again it appeared on the surface and jerked, and again dived beneath the surface... and there, underwater, something suddenly pulled... And I had to pull, only I had to be quick about it!

181

At night, I stretched out, exhausted, in my tent, but no sooner had I closed my eyes and let out a sigh…than I saw the float before my eyes.

I was pleased. It was a pleasant image, I would be able to fall peacefully asleep.

But the float suddenly jerked, then again…jerk, jerk. And I jerked too.

And the same thing went on all night!

Another time I was flying in an airplane when the hum of the engines suddenly changed, and I heard music, as though from a radio, and what ethereal music! An orchestra was playing. The music changed in accordance with my thoughts, it was so harmonious! Then suddenly the hum of the engines changed again, and the divine music disappeared from my head… I was expelled from music school as a child because I had no sense of hearing.

And this time, it was the same thing, just like in the airplane when I heard music, just like when fishing with the float, just like after typing on the typewriter… Only now it was not music, a float, or thoughts like typed letters that were imposing themselves on my brain. This time it was paintings that appeared in my head after my intensive work with paints. And what superb paintings they were!

Evidently the same harmony lives in each and every one of us, but the power to switch on that harmony, our universal talent, depends entirely on what it is that catches our fancy. For a musician, harmony is in music, for a chess player, it is in chess figures, and for the painter, it is found in painting.

Only there should be moderation in everything. You should never force yourself.

I was in a bad way for three days after that creative and alcoholic intoxication. I just could not come back to my senses.

I could not go into the room where my paintings stood. I felt tension and depression.

The smell of paint aroused the fear of hell.

But, thankfully, I finally recovered.

I slept it off, drinking lots of water.

Life blossomed again!

Perhaps that is why people drink, poor things, to find themselves on death's doorstep and then come back to life again, like the seasons of the year.

Maybe the soul needs to live a million little lives as though it were one life, through millions of deaths and resurrections.

My friend Abdullah wrote something similar in one of his poems, saying that life broke down into a thousand tiny pieces, a myriad little lives...

Then it dawned on me. I was not the only one stupid enough to think that God, the Creator, had seen fit to have mercy on me, poor, woeful me suffering in the throes of creativity, and saved me from my plight.

How do you expect Him to have mercy, if He created you as being full of life force, but you, with absolutely no self-respect, decide to destroy yourself in the crudest and most savage way? You, in your own ignorance and barbarism, have confused creation with destruction, with banal primitive overloading!

There is not enough culture. Culture means caring about the life force. There you have it in a nutshell!

I went up to my painting of the bread sitting on the glass. I was filled with a kind of dread, it was hell and not a painting. It was as though it had crawled out of the gutter. It became utterly clear to me that you cannot create anything beautiful and wondrous with a sick soul.

Not one mental breakdown gets away without wreaking material damage, or anguish, anguish over a spoiled painting.

There had been hot and sultry winds in a vibrant yellow and dazzling red desert! What a marvelous painting it had been!

How could I revive that masterpiece now?!

The paint lay in a thick grubby layer on the canvas, the glass and the bread were swamp green, and I, as I remembered shuddering, had also been covered in swamp green paint.

Now my head was clear. But what could I do with yesterday's hell? It was frightening to look at. It drew me into its vortex.

Do not to touch this hell, I told myself. But why was it so scary just to pick up a clean canvas and start painting anew?

I could not do it. It was too scary.

Then I told myself, pluck up your courage and...go for it!

Rakhman had once told me that the more creative texture there is on the canvas in search of the truth, the richer the painting.

The same applies to life itself.

I want to be an artist! I have to finish this painting.

So I picked up my brush and spread that swamp green mass over the entire canvas. I covered everything in swamp green. And suddenly, out of that swamp green color, fir trees arose, and among them, in the same color, but lighter, appeared a circle.

A spot had formed that steeped everything around it in the mystery of a fairytale.

Even though it was lighter, more luminous, it contained all the colors on the canvas, just as a fistful of dirt contains almost the whole of Mendeleev's periodic table. Sunshine!

And clarity appeared! Life! Meaning!

Take care of life!

So culture is a way to reveal the truth without destroying.

Hasai Aliev